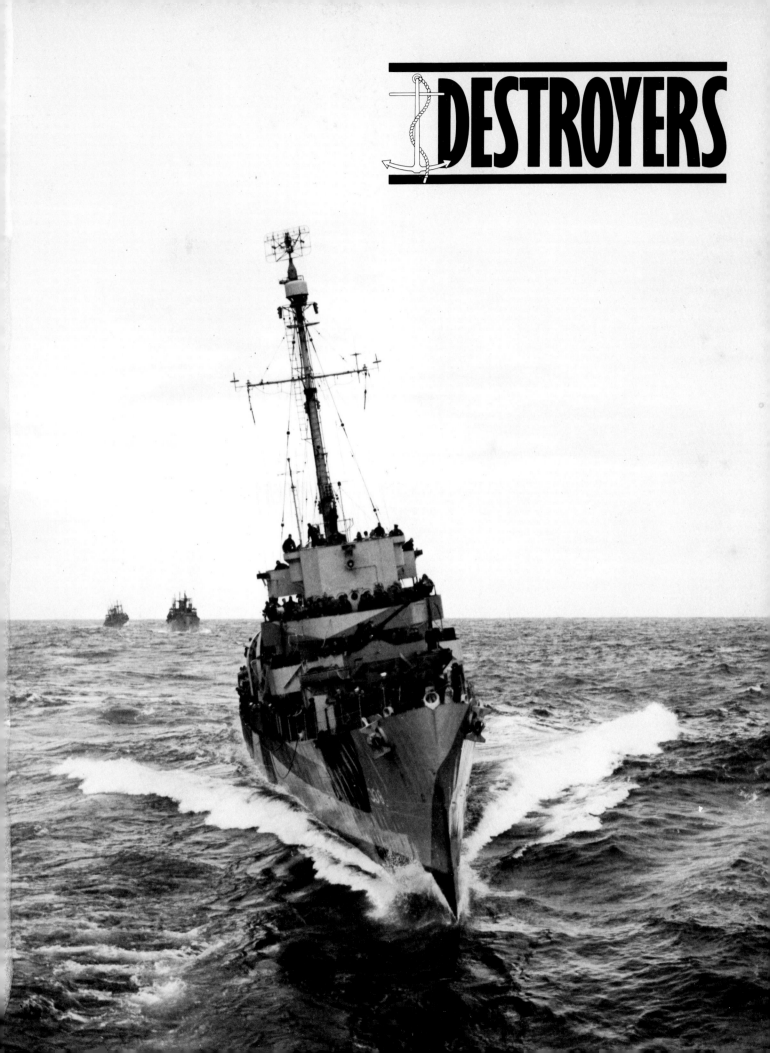

DESTROYERS

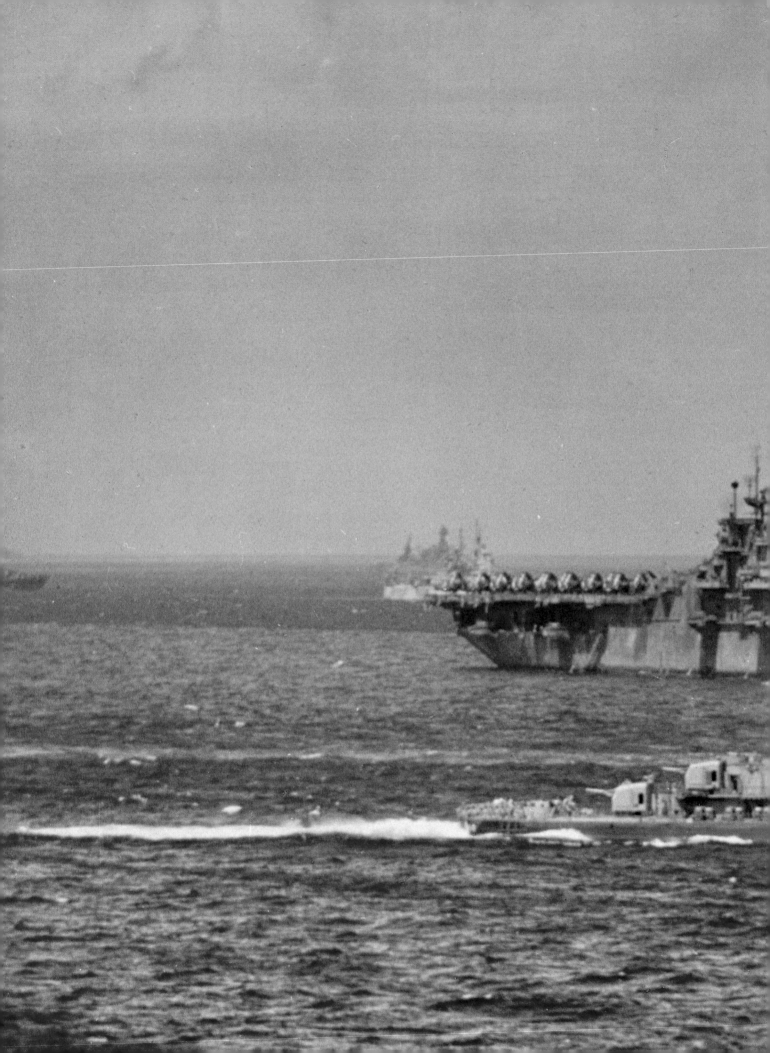

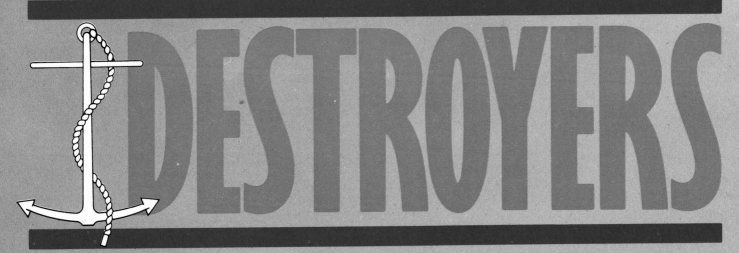

DESTROYERS

ANTONY PRESTON

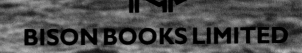

BISON BOOKS LIMITED

First published in 1982 by
Bison Books Inc.
17 Sherwood Place,
Greenwich, CT 06830, USA.

Copyright © 1982 Bison Books Inc

ISBN 0-86124-065-0

Printed in Hong Kong

CONTENTS

DOVER PATROL TO JUTLAND

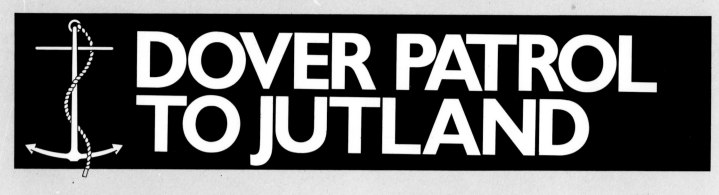

The first shot of the naval war was fired by the British destroyer *Lance* on 5 August 1914, a unit of the 3rd Flotilla, led by the light cruiser *Amphion*.

On receipt of a report that a steamer had been seen 'throwing things overboard' the 3rd Flotilla weighed anchor and left Harwich. At midday they sighted smoke, and the *Lance* and *Landrail* gave chase. The steamer hoisted the German ensign, and was quickly stopped and sunk by the two destroyers. She turned out to be the auxiliary minelayer *Königin Luise*, and she had been caught only 13 hours after the declaration of war. The *Amphion* led her destroyers back to Harwich, but early next morning she ran into the minefield laid by the *Königin Luise*.

Destroyers played a major part in the first big operation of the war, a raid on the German outposts off Heligoland, which led to the Battle of the Heligoland Bight on 28 August. It involved the submarines at Harwich as well as the destroyers. The plan was to use an outer patrol line of submarines to decoy the German torpedo boat patrols out to sea, where they could be trapped by the Harwich Force destroyers and their light cruiser leaders. Both sides had a lot to learn. First the British betrayed their intentions by sending too many radio messages, and then poor staffwork at the Admiralty prevented the two commodores, Keyes and Tyrwhitt, from being told that the Admiralty had decided to send more powerful reinforcements, in the shape of a cruiser squadron and four battlecruisers. The Germans, on the other hand, were caught completely unawares, and their heavy units were lying in the Jade River without steam up and unable to cross the bar until high tide. It had not occurred to the Ger-

man High Command that the British would send such strong forces into the Bight, almost within range of the guns on Heligoland, and their light forces were at a disadvantage.

At about 0700 the *Laurel* opened fire on the German *G.194* and within an hour British destroyers and the light cruisers *Arethusa* and *Fearless* were in action with the torpedo boats guarding the German inner patrol line. Destroyer gunfire could never be very accurate, and although the range fell to 7000 yards the thick haze meant that the heavy fire was largely ineffective. Suddenly the cruisers *Stettin* and *Frauenlob*, which had been lying at anchor off Heligoland and had raised steam when they heard the gunfire, arrived on the scene. They took on the British cruisers and were able to silence the *Arethusa* with 35 hits. The British destroyers left the cruisers to fight it out, and concentrated on punishing the torpedo boats *D.8* and *T.33*, which had found themselves caught up in the battle. The *Fearless* and her destroyers later managed to trap the *V.187*, which went down fighting.

The *Arethusa* had been badly knocked about, and although the sweep should have been over, at 1030 her destroyers were still standing by while she stopped to make urgent repairs to her machinery and guns. Every minute that passed made it more likely that German reinforcements would appear from the Ems and Jade. When the first of these appeared, the light cruiser *Strassburg*, she was mistaken for a much larger cruiser and Commodore Tyrwhitt signalled to Vice-Admiral Beatty and his battlecruisers, 'Respectfully submit that I may be supported. Am hard pressed.' But long before any help could arrive the

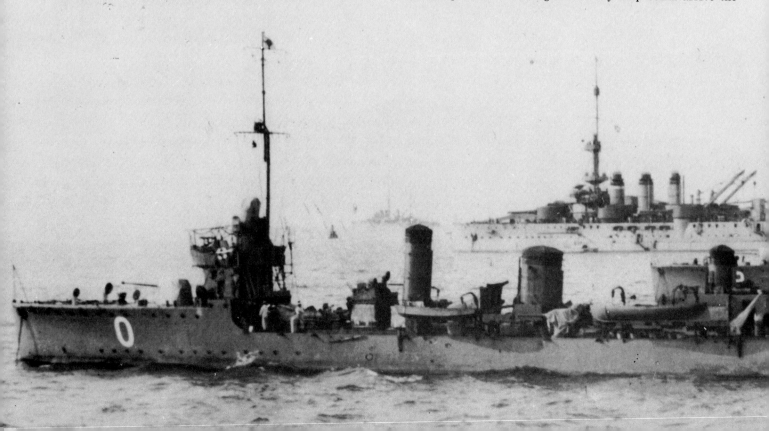

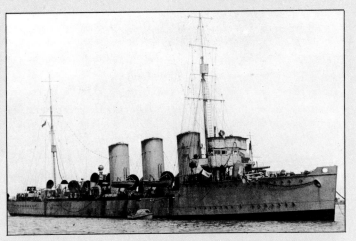

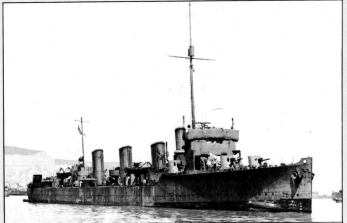

destroyers would have to face heavy punishment. Just as the *Laurel* turned away after firing her torpedoes a salvo of 10.5-cm shells hit her. One hit in the engine-room killed four men and injured others; a second hit near the forward 4-inch gun killed most of the crew and another wrecked the after funnel and wounded her captain. Her next astern, the *Liberty*, lost her captain and signalman when a shell burst behind the bridge, and the last in line, the *Laertes*, was hit in the boiler-room.

Suddenly the cruiser *Mainz* shuddered as one of the British torpedoes hit her. In total darkness, with every piece of glass between decks smashed, the ship began to sink slowly by the head. She had already been set on fire, and the arrival of the first British reinforcements, a squadron of light cruisers, sealed her fate. The *Arethusa* was still limping home at 10 knots, and it seemed that she might yet be cut off and sunk, as the German reinforcements were now arriving. But suddenly five large ships came into sight from the west. They were Admiral Beatty's battlecruisers, the *Lion*, *Princess Royal*, *Queen Mary*, *Invincible* and *New Zealand*, steaming at full speed, with dense clouds of coal-smoke billowing from their funnels.

Heading between the burning wreck of the *Mainz* and the *Arethusa* the big ships turned their guns on the *Köln* and brought her to a stop. Then the luckless *Ariadne* blundered out of the mist and crossed the *Lion*'s bows, to be shattered by

Above left: HMS *Swift* at Dover. She was the flotilla leader in a frantic action against German torpedo boats in the Channel in 1917.
Above: HMS *Broke* was also involved in the action and rammed and sank a German torpedo boat.

repeated hits. Pausing only to finish off the *Köln*, the battle-cruisers drew off to cover the light forces' withdrawal.

It had been a risky action, but the risks had been justified by the bold handling of the British destroyers, which had repeatedly held off light cruisers and had saved the *Arethusa* from being sunk. It was to be the last major destroyer action for nearly two years, but the Harwich Force in particular was to be embroiled in many skirmishes with the opposing German cruisers and destroyers through the next four years. However much time the big ships on both sides might spend in harbor, the destroyers were constantly in action. The Harwich Force became more and more important as the chief offensive squadron in the North Sea, well placed to intercept raids by German surface ships and to mount offensive patrols in the southern North Sea.

The other important squadron was the Dover Patrol, which was based on Dover to guard the vital cross-Channel supply route between Britain and France. As the armies on the Western Front expanded, an ever-increasing number of troops had to be transported across the Channel, accompanied by vast quantities

Below: In the Mediterranean German and Austrian pressure forced the Allies to call in whatever help was available. These Japanese destroyers are lying off Corfu, April 1917.

of war material such as coal for French industry and ammunition for the guns. In the first weeks, when German troops swept through Belgium, the Dover Patrol destroyers showed how adaptable they were by joining in the bombardments of the German right flank.

The cross-Channel convoys were a tempting target for raids by German torpedo boats, particularly when the Germans were able to establish forward bases at Zeebrugge and Ostend. Fortunately for the Allies the northern French port of Dunkirk was still on their hands, and it became an equally useful forward base. Some idea of the problem, and also the size of target presented, is indicated by the fact that the average number of cross-Channel sailings was about 700 each year. Between August 1914 and December 1917 nearly six million troops were carried in addition to some 120,000 east-west transits of the English Channel. During the same period a further 800,000 casualties

were brought back from France. Yet, in all this time only one hospital ship and an empty transport were mined and another empty transport was sunk by German torpedo boats. The other casualties were all sustained by the warships and small patrol craft.

The most famous action of the Dover Patrol occurred on the night of 20 April 1917, when two large destroyers intercepted a force of German torpedo boats in the Channel. The flotilla leader *Swift* and the ex-Chilean *Broke* were patrolling off Dover when they heard firing off Calais and saw gun-flashes. When shells began to fall on Dover they knew for certain that a raid was in progress; they steered for Calais, but took care not to be drawn away from what they rightly interpreted as the enemy's main objective, the large collection of shipping which was sheltering in the Downs. In fact two large torpedo boats had bombarded Calais to draw off the patrols while four more had slipped in to bombard Dover before joining forces again.

About seven miles east of Dover the *Swift* and *Broke* sighted six vessels steaming fast off the port bow in the opposite direction. The strangers opened fire and the two British boats replied immediately. The *Swift* put her helm hard over to ram, but Commander Peck and his staff on the bridge were dazzled by the flash of the 6-inch gun forward and she passed just astern of the German line, firing a single torpedo as she went. Commander Evans, astern in the *Broke*, held his fire to allow the torpedo director a clear moment to aim. This torpedo or the one fired by the *Swift* a moment earlier, hit the *G.85* full amidships in a huge plume of smoke and spray. Evans, seeing his intended victim hit, altered course to ram the torpedo boat astern. It was the *G.42*, and she tried frantically to escape with sparks pouring from her funnels but her captain had left it too late, and with a screech of grinding steel the *Broke*'s bow tore into the thin side plating and flung her over on her beam ends.

Above right: The ill-fated Allied landings at Gallipoli in 1915 suffered from extended lines of supply. Here, HMS *Wolverine* guards the transports at 'W' Beach.
Right: Destroyers could be uncomfortable in rough weather but the task of protecting the Fleet had to be continued. Royal Navy 'M' Class destroyers escort a squadron of the Grand Fleet.

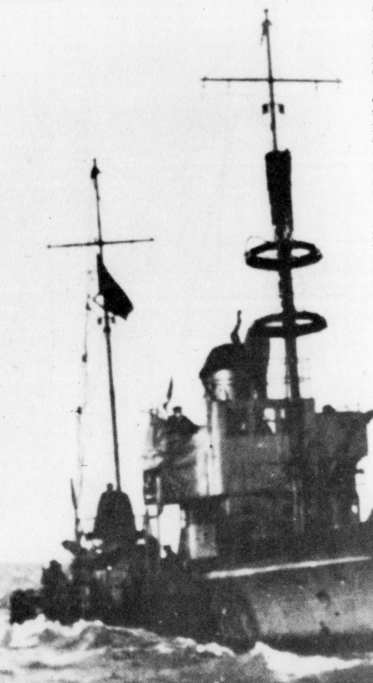

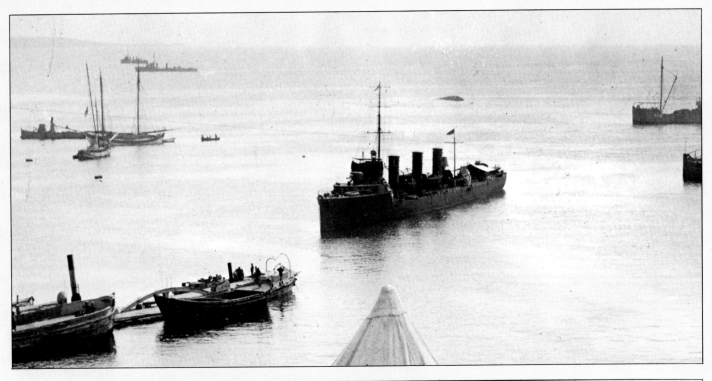

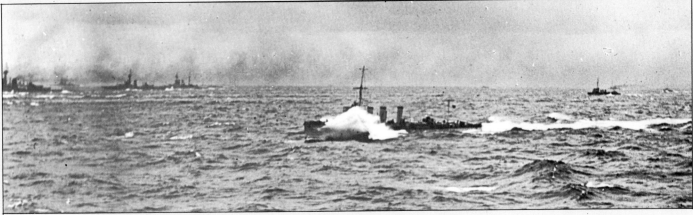

Below: German torpedo boats were a constant threat to the troop and supply ships which steamed back and forth across the Channel. However, they managed to sink only one transport during the war, thanks largely to the efforts of the destroyers of the Dover Patrol.

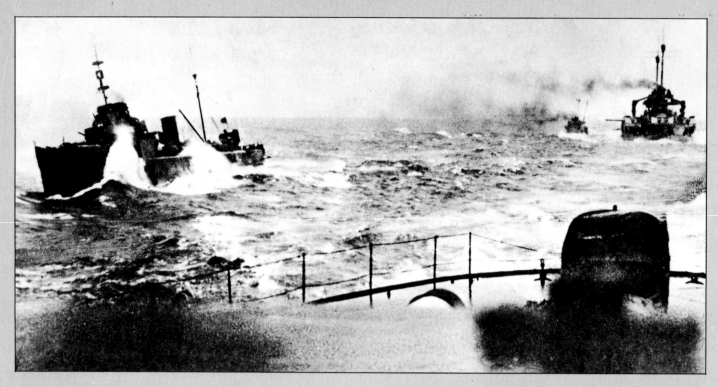

Above: German torpedo boats, with their low freeboard, also fared badly in a rough sea.

It must have been a nightmare scene, with the *Broke*'s guns pouring shells into *G.42* at point-blank range. Several of the German seamen had clambered onto the forecastle of the British destroyer, and the survivors of the forward gun crews assumed that they were boarders and armed themselves with rifles, bayonets and cutlasses. A murderous fight took place, at a range so close that even the officers on the bridge were using their personal side-arms. The *Broke* herself was in danger, for a box of cordite cartridges was burning, and illuminating her in a lurid red glow. One of the surviving German torpedo boats slid past out of the darkness and fired shells indiscriminately into the inferno. In seconds the *Broke*'s decks were running with blood, as a quarter of her crew were killed or wounded by 10.5-cm shells.

With her bows still locked into the hull of the sinking German

torpedo boat she was a sitting target until the unknown torpedo boat disappeared. Painfully she ground her way clear and tried to follow the *Swift*, which was in full pursuit of two enemy torpedo boats, but a shell had damaged the main steam pipe and soon she was losing feed-water to the boilers, so she steamed slowly back to the scene of the action. The *Swift* was soon back, for she had also been damaged severely by shellfire, and could not maintain full speed. It had been a brief and bloody engagement, but two large torpedo boats had been sunk and it effectively put an end to raids from the Flanders torpedo boat flotillas for the time being. Both commanders were awarded the DSO, and 'Evans of the *Broke*' rose to become a colorful Admiral in later years.

The destroyer's most valuable contribution in World War I was her unexpected efficiency as an antisubmarine craft. Until specially-designed escorts were built only the destroyer had the speed, maneuverability and armament to sink a submarine before she submerged.

The threat from submarines had not been taken seriously in

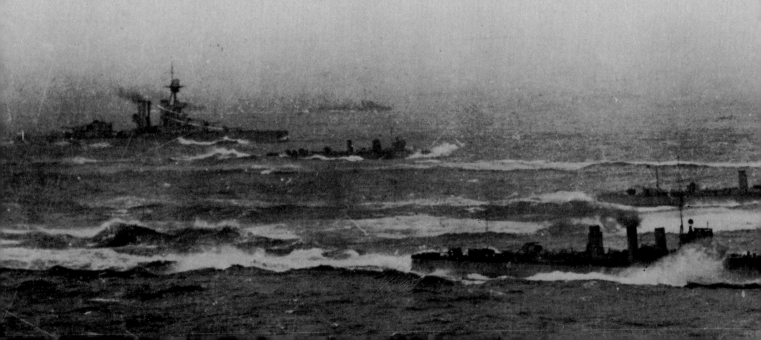

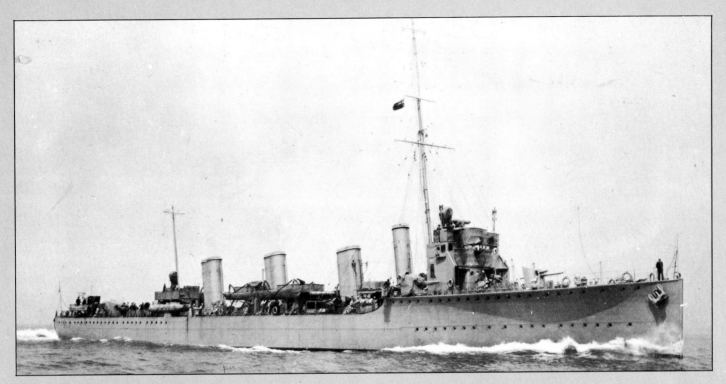

Above: HMS *Tipperary* took part in the night action at Jutland. She was a flotilla leader built for the Chilean Navy but taken over by the Admiralty at the beginning of the war.

the early weeks of the war, but after several large ships had been torpedoed it was realized that no formation of warships should move anywhere without an escort of destroyers. After the inconclusive Battle of the Dogger Bank early in 1915, in which the destroyers had little to do but finish off the battered German cruiser *Blücher*, their work became almost entirely monotonous patrolling.

There was the ever-present danger from mines and the risk of collision between ships maneuvering at high speed in fog or darkness, without lights or radar. Out of 67 British destroyers lost between 1914 and 1918, collisions accounted for 18 and another 12 were wrecked.

The great trial of strength between the British Grand Fleet and the German High Seas Fleet eventually came at the end of May 1916. The Battle of Jutland was the first and in a sense the only test of the theories of destroyer tactics, for both sides had large numbers of torpedo craft present; 80 British destroyers and flotilla leaders and 62 German torpedo boats. The battle divided itself into two distinct parts, the day action on 31 May, in which

the rival torpedo craft duelled with one another in vain attempts to take the pressure off their capital ships, and the night action on 31 May–1 June, in which British destroyers faced the entire German Fleet alone.

It was two German torpedo boats, *B.109* and *B.110* which unwittingly started the battle. At about 1600 they were ordered to examine a small Danish steamer, and while they were doing so two British light cruisers arrived on the same mission. Shots were fired and each group returned to its main body flashing the message 'Enemy in sight.' A fierce action developed between Admiral Beatty's battlecruisers and the German battlecruisers under Admiral Hipper, and when the British lost HMS *Indefatigable* and the flagship *Lion* was badly hit, the destroyers were ordered to attack to relieve the pressure. At almost the same time 15 German torpedo boats were ordered to attack the

Below: Battleships of the Grand Fleet are escorted by the 11th Destroyer Flotilla. HMS *Marmion* is followed by *Marne, Prince, Kempenfelt* and *Morning Star*.

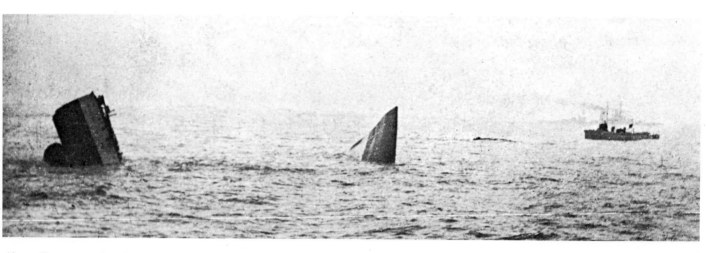

Above: Destroyers played a vital role in the Battle of Jutland (1916) with 80 taking part. Here HMS *Badger* approaches the wreck of the battlecruiser *Invincible*.

British capital ships, as Hipper's line was coming under heavy fire. A fierce action developed in 'no man's land' between the two battle lines, in which the British *Nestor* and *Nomad* and the German *V.27* and *V.29* were crippled and left in a sinking condition. But the British destroyers' heavy gun-armament enabled them to keep the German boats off, and forced them to fire their torpedoes at too great a range to score any hits. The British destroyers fired their torpedoes at a range of 5000–7000 yards, and although most were dodged by a timely turn away by Hipper, one from the *Petard* exploded against the armor of the *Seydlitz*, tearing a hole 13 by 39 feet in her side. Although taking in water, she was able to keep her place in the battle line.

In the next phase of the day-action the two battlecruiser forces fell back on their main fleets. Visibility was deteriorating, partly because of haze but mainly from the dense clouds of smoke from the scores of coal-burning ships present. Both commanders were holding their light forces in check, knowing that a general fleet action was imminent, but this did not prevent HMS *Onslow* from attacking the cruiser *Wiesbaden* on her own initiative. Lieutenant-Commander John Tovey (a future Commander in Chief of the Home Fleet) decided that the damaged cruiser was a 'target of opportunity' and approached her. Suddenly he saw enemy ships looming out of the haze and realized that his destroyer was only 8000 yards from Admiral Hipper's battlecruisers. Tovey was unperturbed and turned to fire his four torpedoes at them, but just as the first torpedo leapt from its tube a heavy-caliber shell hit the *Onslow* in the boiler-room. With steam billowing from No. 2 boiler-room and her speed dropping rapidly, the *Onslow* limped past the *Wiesbaden* and fired a second torpedo, which exploded under the cruiser's conning tower. Then Tovey saw a line of battleships, Admiral Scheer's High Seas Fleet, deploying into action, and decided that the destruction of one destroyer was worth the chance of scoring a torpedo-hit. Although making only ten knots and listing heavily the 1000-ton *Onslow* crawled across the sea and launched her last two torpedoes at a range of 8000 yards.

It would be pleasing to report that such heroism was rewarded by at least one torpedo-hit on a battleship, but both the *Onslow*'s torpedoes missed, and her hit on the *Wiesbaden* did not prevent that sorely battered ship from continuing the fight later. The destroyer eventually came to a dead stop when her boilers ran out of feed-water. For a time it looked as if she might be sunk by the German ships, which were within gun-range, and her anxious crew had a grandstand view of an action between the battleship *Warspite* and the head of the German line, but the battleships swept on and ignored her. She was eventually taken in tow by her fellow-destroyer HMS *Defender*, which had the dubious distinction of having an unexploded 12-inch shell in the ashpit of one of her boilers. The two cripples fell in with the

damaged *Warspite*, making her way back to Rosyth, but the battleship dared not loiter to help the destroyers, and left them. After a nightmare journey across 350 miles in a rising sea the two ships arrived safely. Both captains received the DSO, Tovey for his gallant attack and Commander Palmer of the *Defender* for his outstanding seamanship and determination.

Meanwhile the Grand Fleet was deploying into action, and Admiral Jellicoe, the Commander in Chief, pushed his three battlecruisers, *Invincible*, *Indomitable* and *Inflexible*, forward to support Beatty's ships. Escorting these ships were four destroyers, led by Commander Loftus W Jones in HMS *Shark*. The *Shark* and *Acasta* attacked a German light cruiser and a battlecruiser with torpedoes, but the divisional leader was badly damaged by gunfire. Refusing a tow from the *Acasta*, Loftus Jones was preparing to abandon ship when two German torpedo boats appeared. Although only the midships 4-inch gun was still working the crippled *Shark* fought back until she was hit by a torpedo. A handful of men, including the desperately wounded captain escaped on a raft, but during the night he and eight others died, leaving only six survivors out of a ship's company of 77 officers and men. The *Acasta* narrowly escaped the same fate, but she was towed by another destroyer and made port.

As darkness fell the fleet action died away, leaving the British apparently well placed between the High Seas Fleet and its bases. The capital ships were grouped into cruising formation once more, to provide a more compact defense against a night attack by torpedo boats, which was expected. Admiral Jellicoe stationed his destroyers five miles astern of the main fleet, partly to screen his big ships against such an attack but also to give them the opportunity to attack the enemy fleet if it should pass to the south on its way home. But these destroyers had very little idea of the whereabouts of much of their own fleet, let alone the enemy, apart from the knowledge that the battle fleet was five miles ahead. In the confusion of the fighting that had just ended the staff had overlooked the fact that the destroyers had no way of knowing whether they were attacking friend or foe. If they flashed the recognition signal they could expect to be lashed by gunfire, and if they fired first they ran the awful risk of sinking one of their own ships. The truth of the matter was, of course, that no-one had ever imagined such a large number of destroyers gathered together, with so little concrete information about everybody's position.

To summarize, the High Sea Fleet decided to take its chance in a night action, and try to drive its way through the screen of destroyers. In this decision Scheer had been helped by two strokes of good fortune: an intercepted signal told him that the destroyers were well astern of Jellicoe's fleet, and a rash visual exchange of the night challenge and reply between two British

Right: The US shipbuilding industry broke all construction records in 1918. Here USS *Belknap* (DD.251) makes a high speed trial.
Far right: In 1918 HMS *Walker* was one of the new 'V & W' Class which was much imitated by other navies.

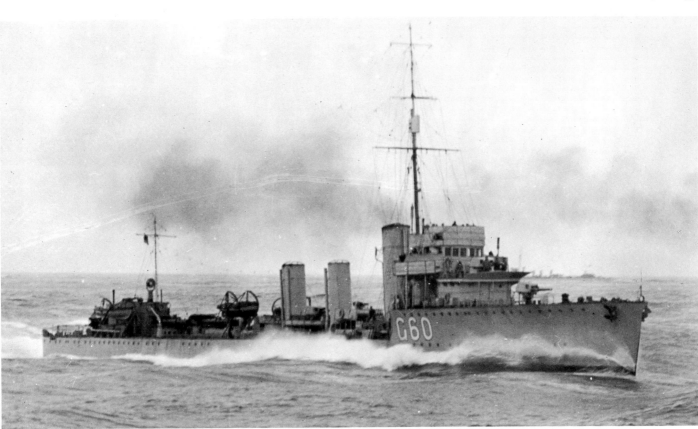

Above: The flotilla leader *Anzac* at high speed.

battlecruisers at dusk had been partially read by a German light cruiser. The first piece of information gave Scheer the assurance that he was only facing light forces, against which the German night-fighting organization had more than a fair chance of success, and the second meant that British ships would be dangerously unsure in those vital opening minutes of night action, whereas the Germans would know immediately that they had been challenged by an enemy ship.

The first clash came at 2205, when the 11th Flotilla was challenged by ships which gave the first two letters of the challenge for the day, followed by two incorrect letters. Before anyone could decide what to do, searchlights were unmasked by the cruisers *Hamburg* and *Elbing*, followed by a withering fire. The light cruiser *Castor* fired back, and she and two of her destroyers each fired a torpedo, but the rest of the flotilla held their fire, convinced that a mistake had been made. The torpedoes missed and the two hostile cruisers disappeared into the darkness as rapidly as they had appeared.

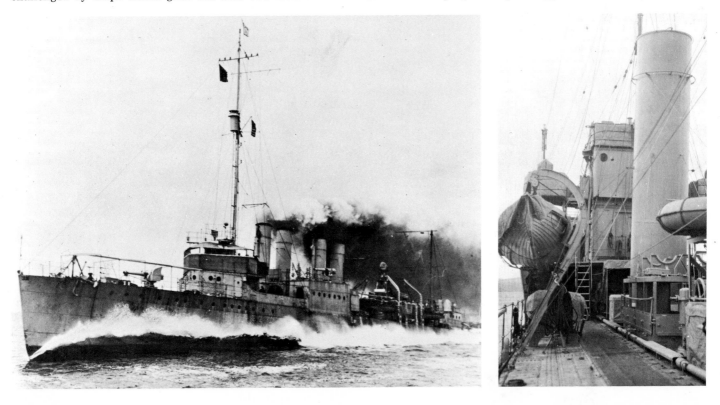

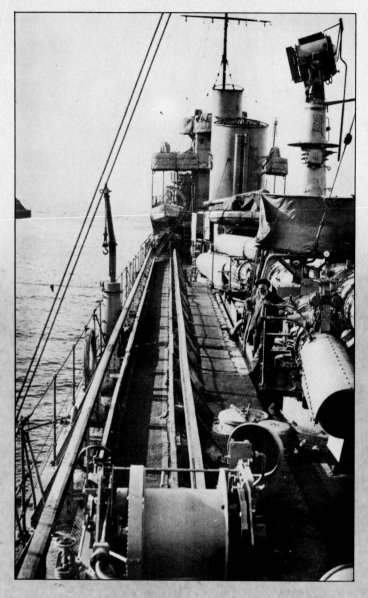

The leader *Tipperary* and her 4th Flotilla had seen the gun flashes and searchlights of the *Castor's* action, and so were alerted. This was not enough, however, for as soon as the *Tipperary* challenged what she mistook for a force of friendly cruisers, she was blasted by gunfire. The 4th Flotilla had in fact run into the head of the German battle fleet, and the puny destroyers were about to take on dreadnoughts 20 times their size. The *Spitfire* swung to starboard to avoid the blazing wreck of the *Tipperary*, but her captain was blinded by the searchlights, and failed to see the ram bow of a big ship looming overhead. To avoid being cut in half he chose to collide with his opponent, port bow to port bow, and the *Spitfire* ground down the side of the other ship. The big ship's forward turret swung round and fired a salvo at her, but the destroyer was so small that the shells roared overhead; even so, the blast was enough to flatten the bridge and demolish the mast and fore-funnel.

When the *Spitfire* drew clear she had on board 20 feet of steel plating and part of some anchor gear wedged into her messdeck. Lieutenant-Commander Trelawny thought that the enemy 'light cruiser' was probably not a new ship because of the thick paint, but his opponent was actually the dreadnought battleship *Nassau*, displacing 20,000 tons and armed with twelve 11-inch guns.

The German ships were not having it all their own way, and the head of their line was thrown into confusion as a result of the British destroyers' torpedo attacks. The *Elbing* was one of a number of cruisers which were forced to weave between the battleships in an attempt to dodge the torpedoes, and while doing this she was rammed by the *Posen*. Then the *Rostock* did the same, and was hit by a torpedo as she squeezed through astern of the *Westfalen*. But the 4th Flotilla had been destroyed as a fighting formation without being able to stop the High Seas Fleet's breakthrough. Four destroyers had been sunk and four more seriously damaged while 390 officers and men had been killed, and 72 wounded.

The next obstacle in Admiral Scheer's path was a mixed force of destroyers, mainly the 13th Flotilla, and some of the 9th and 10th Flotillas. Although casualties were not as heavy as in the 4th Flotilla, the German battle-line again smashed its way through, damaging the *Petard* severely and literally blowing the *Turbulent* apart with gunfire, without suffering any loss. Then the 12th Flotilla attacked, and this time one of their torpedoes found its mark. Suddenly the predreadnought battleship *Pom-*

Above left: Destroyers were used as fast minelayers. Here a stoker contemplates the port mine-rail of HMS *Walker*.
Below: The arrival of US destroyers at Queenstown, Ireland, in May 1917 greatly helped spread the load of convoy duties. USS *Davis* (DD.65) is the leading ship.

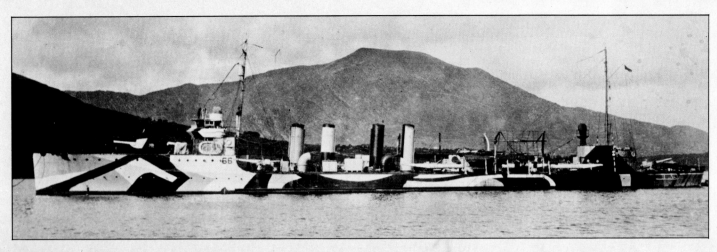

Above: USS *Allen* (DD.66) was typical of the American destroyers of World War I. She also saw service in World War II.

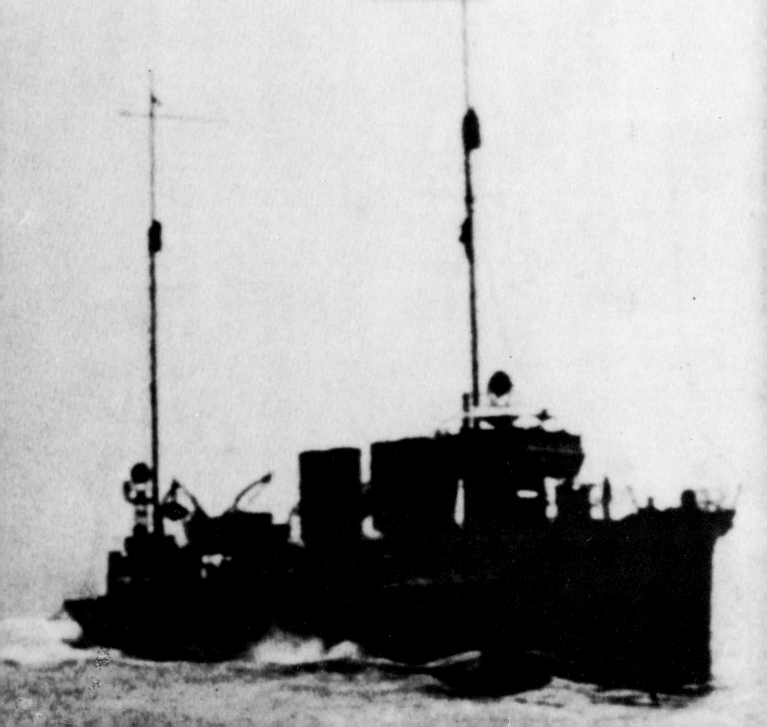

mern of the 2nd Squadron was illuminated by a flash which spread along her waterline. She heeled over, torn apart by a series of further explosions, and quickly disappeared in flames as her ammunition detonated. All 844 men on board were lost.

Jutland showed that the destroyers had been overrated. Although both Commanders in Chief had repeatedly turned away rather than face torpedo attacks, the gunfire of defending cruisers and the battleships themselves had been sufficient to drive off daylight attacks. At night destroyers had found it very difficult to operate against a well-coordinated defense. There were 252 warships present at the battle, and of these only the German *Seydlitz* and the British *Marlborough* were damaged by torpedoes in daylight, while night attacks had accounted for two light cruisers and the old *Pommern*.

For many years the experience of Jutland was to dominate destroyer tactics in all navies, which is why the fighting has been described at some length. What the British learned was that, above all, each group of destroyers must be given as much information as possible about dispositions of both friendly and hostile ships. The second lesson was that flotillas were too large, as had been predicted as long ago as 1887. The large flotilla was retained for the time being as an administrative unit but for tactical purposes it was broken down into two divisions of eight. There was to be no second meeting between the British and German Fleets, and the growing need to divert destroyers to hunting U-Boats meant that any serious revision of destroyer tactics had to be deferred.

By the time of the second unrestricted U-Boat campaign of 1917 destroyers had become indispensible as escorts. Hitherto formations of warships had always moved with their screen of destroyers, but now merchant ships needed escorting as well when convoys were introduced in May 1917. Thus, when the United States entered the war the US Navy was asked to send destroyers as the most urgent priority, and a Japanese offer to send eight of their own to the Mediterranean was gratefully accepted.

On 24 April 1917 six destroyers of the US Atlantic Fleet, the *Wadsworth*, *Conyngham*, *Porter*, *McDougal*, *Davis* and *Wainwright* weighed anchor and left for Europe. They were the first massive reinforcement sent by the US Navy, and they were to prove crucial. Only 26 destroyers had been authorized between 1911 and 1914, and it was out of this group that the first reinforcements for Europe were drawn. In the interim a new type of destroyer was laid down, based on the 1913–14 designs but with a flush deck from bow to stern to give greater longitudinal strength, in place of the conventional raised forecastle. Although the last 50 of this giant program were not completed by the Armistice, the rate at which the others were built meant that they were all in time.

In World War I destroyers changed rapidly from being small, specialized craft to a warship type which was an integral part of the fleet. No other type proved so adaptable to the changes brought about by submarine and mine warfare, and no other type saw so much action. In every navy destroyers were hardworked and indispensable. Valuable lessons had been learned about design and methods of employment, but above all a tradition of bravery, skill and determination had been forged in battle.

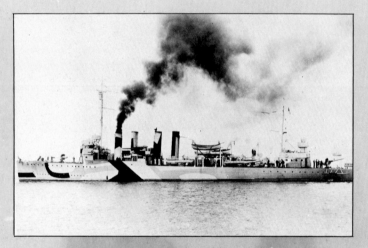

Above: Completed in 1918, USS *Ward* was the first US warship in action in the Pacific in World War II when she sank two Japanese midget submarines just off Pearl Harbor, before the air attack.
Below: *V.99* was a large 1200-ton German destroyer, seen here on trials.

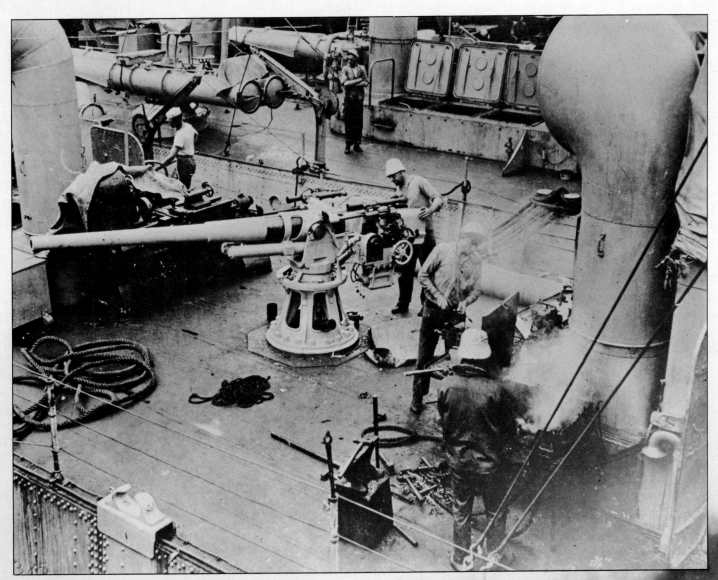

Above: The Queenstown base allowed the US Navy to carry out maintenance without returning to the USA. A spare part for a 4-inch gun is made on a portable forge.

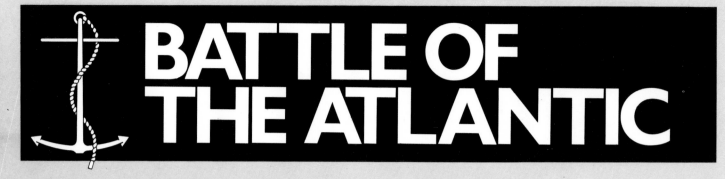

BATTLE OF THE ATLANTIC

The naval war began in earnest only hours after the expiry of the Anglo-French ultimatum to Germany on the morning of 3 September 1939. Two weeks later, on 14 September, the new carrier HMS *Ark Royal* was cruising in the Western Approaches with a hunting group of four destroyers. Suddenly tracks passed close astern of the carrier as *U.39* fired a salvo of four torpedoes. The destroyers pounced, and their Asdics soon picked up the echo of the U-Boat; after a short hunt the U-Boat was destroyed, the first of many to fall to destroyers. Three days later, however, the carrier *Courageous* was sunk by *U.29* in very similar circumstances, and her destroyers failed to find the attacker.

German destroyers played an important part in the seizure of Narvik on 9 April 1940. With a mixture of treachery and bluff 10 of them entered the fjord to land troops, and parleyed with the Norwegian ships defending the harbor. Commodore Bonte's flagship, the *Wilhelm Heidkamp*, broke off negotiations and without warning fired two torpedoes into the old coast defense battleship *Eidsvold*; a few minutes later the *Bernd von Arnim* put seven more into the *Norge*. But Bonte's flotilla was not to be allowed to savor its easy victory for long, for the British 2nd Destroyer Flotilla was already on its way, four H Class boats led by Captain Bernard Warburton-Lee in the flotilla leader *Hardy*. Warburton-Lee knew that Narvik was in German hands, and had decided to attack the transports, but he only knew of six destroyers, rather than the 10 which were actually there. The weather was atrocious with continuous snow squalls and poor visibility, but it allowed the five British destroyers to reach Narvik by 0400 on 10 April without being spotted.

At 0430 three of the destroyers swept into action, taking the Germans completely by surprise. No sooner had the alarm sounded than a torpedo hit the *Wilhelm Heidkamp* killing the Commodore and sinking her. Two more torpedoes blew the *Anton Schmidt* in half and shells damaged the *Diether von Roeder* and *Hans Lüdemann*. All five destroyers came in a second time and shot up the transports, but a third attack ran out of luck. Lieutenant-Commander Erich Bey had been given sufficient warning to get his three destroyers out of the neighboring Herjangs Fjord, while further down the main fjord Lieutenant-Commander Fritz Berger brought out the remaining two to cut off the British retreat. Warburton-Lee's destroyers were now caught between two fires. A 5-inch shell wrecked the *Hardy*'s bridge and killed Warburton-Lee, and then the ship ran aground out of control. The *Hunter* was also sunk and the *Hotspur* badly damaged, but the *Hostile* and *Havock* turned back to support their flotilla-mates. The German destroyers were also being hit, however, and were unable to prevent the crippled *Hotspur* from escaping. Even though two British destroyers had been sunk Warburton-Lee's attack had sealed

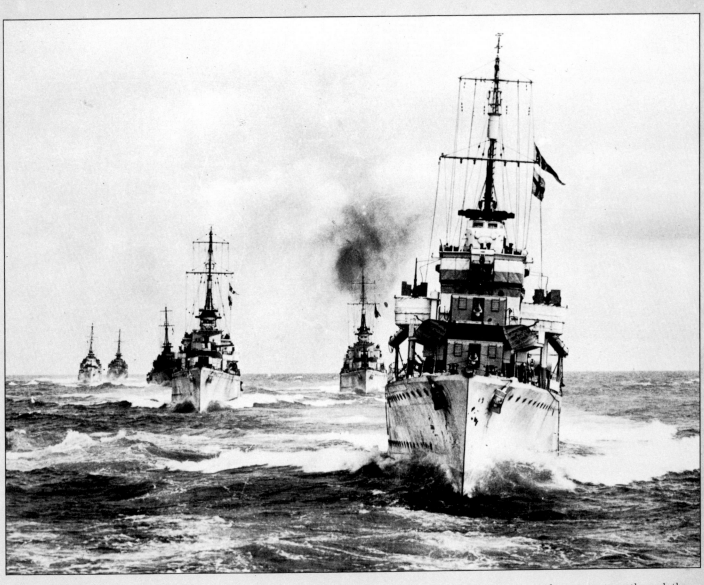

Above: The Royal Navy goes to war as destroyers steam through the waters of the North Sea in line.
Below: The veteran 'V & W' Class HMS *Walker* showed that she still had her teeth when she sank *U.99* and captured her ace commander, K/Lt Otto Kretschmer, in Spring 1944.

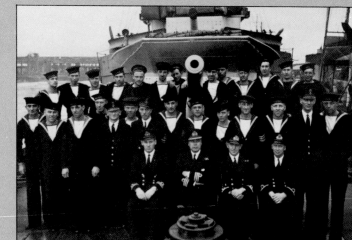

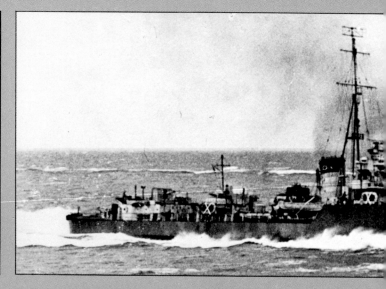

Above: In 1943 HMS *Vanoc* had already been at sea for 25 years. Her captain and some of her officers and crew pose for a Silver Jubilee photograph.

the fate of the eight German destroyers left at Narvik. On the way down the fjord HMS *Havock* sank an ammunition ship bringing 5-inch shells for the German flotilla, and as they had fired away nearly all their ammunition and torpedoes they were now unable to face further action with any hope of success.

On 13 April the blow fell. Vice-Admiral Whitworth, flying his flag in the battleship *Warspite*, was ordered to recapture Narvik and wipe out the remaining enemy destroyers. Taking nine destroyers with her, the battleship thrust up Narvik Fjord, with her floatplane reconnoitering for the destroyers and using her 15 inch guns with terrible effect. The destroyer *Eskimo* had her bows blown off by a torpedo but all eight of the German flotilla were sunk. The two Battles of Narvik did more than finish off the destroyers which had taken Narvik; with 10

destroyers sunk, the *Kriegsmarine* destroyer-strength was now reduced to nine vessels, and in the precarious months after Dunkirk, when the German Naval Staff was asked to support the Army's Sealion invasion plan, lack of destroyers to screen the big ships was one of the most crucial problems. Three of them were still under repair in August 1940, leaving only six destroyers to face the Royal Navy in the English Channel.

The Royal Navy had 162 destroyers left after the evacuation from France but only 74 of these were undamaged. The British Prime Minister had already asked the United States' President to consider lending 50 of the old flush-deckers to tide the RN over until its big building program began to produce new destroyers in 1941, but now destroyers were desperately needed to fight off the threatened invasion of the British Isles. On 5 September the two governments agreed to the exchange: 50 old destroyers in return for a 99-year lease on bases in British territory abroad. Captain Taprell Dorling ('Taffrail') is credited with the happy idea of naming the ships after towns common to

Below: Although built to fill an order for Brazil, HMS *Havant* was taken on by the Royal Navy when war broke out. She was sunk by German bombs off the Dunkirk beaches in May 1940.

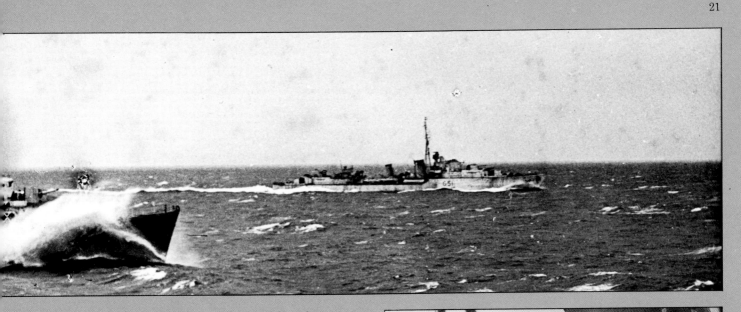

Above: Flotilla leader HMS *Onslow* and the Tribal Class destroyer *Ashanti*.
Right: The distinctive four funnels of a flush-decked ex-United States, Lease-Lend destroyer.

the USA and the United Kingdom, but to the RN they were always known as the 'four-pipers.' They were delivered to the Canadian base at Halifax, Nova Scotia, and there they were commissioned into the RN and the Canadian Navy.

Despite the grumbles the British and Canadians achieved a lot with their flush-deckers. Several accounted for the sinking of U-Boats in the Battle of the Atlantic and on 28 March 1942 the *Campbeltown* (ex-USS *Buchanan*) was used to blow up the giant Normandie dock at St Nazaire to deny it to the battleship *Tirpitz*. Eight were lost, including one lent to the Soviet Navy in 1944. Toward the end of the war they were reduced to humbler duties, often serving as training ships or aircraft targets.

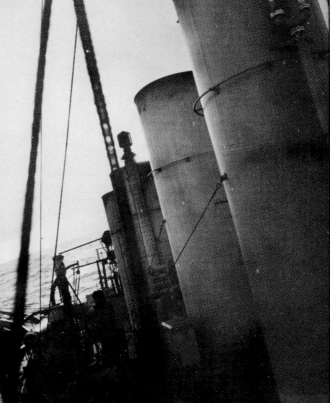

H32

The Battle of the Atlantic was the most gruelling test for destroyers, whether ancient flush-deckers, their British veteran equivalents, the 'V&Ws', or the latest fleet destroyers. The winter conditions varied from grim to fearful, and tested human endurance to its limits. Although destroyers were effective submarine hunters they were far from ideal for the task. Even in normal weather they were lively, and would 'roll on wet grass'; in foul weather their slim bows tended to plough through waves rather than lift to them, so that they were battered far more than the tubby little corvettes and trawlers. Life under such conditions was endured but nothing more, and the only consolation was that the U-Boats were equally hampered by bad weather.

The transfer of 50 destroyers to the RN in 1940 was only the beginning of the United States' involvement in World War II. In March 1941 the Lend-Lease Bill was enacted to allow more warships to be built and 'lent' to the RN to ease the shortage of escorts. In April the Defense Zone, in which US freighters could be escorted regardless of whether they were carrying war material to Britain or not, was extended to longitude 26 degrees West. In the middle of the year the US Government took responsibility for guaranteeing the 'neutrality' of Iceland by putting American troops in place of the British and Canadians who had been there for a year. As Iceland was used by British and Canadian warships for refuelling there was now the likelihood of a U-Boat mistaking a USN destroyer for a hostile escort. The flush-decker's distinctive silhouette was common to both navies, and the latest *Benson* and *Bristol* Classes were similar in general build and layout to the British 'A to I' types.

From the spring of 1941 three destroyer squadrons were operating in the North Atlantic, DesRons 7, 30 and 31. The first 'hostile' action seems to have been an attack on a sonar contact by the destroyer *Niblack* in April, but the first serious provocation was the '*Greer* Incident' on 4 September 1941. The old flush-decker belonged to DesRon 30 but was proceeding independently, carrying supplies and mail to Reykjavik, when a British maritime patrol aircraft signalled to warn her that a U-Boat had been sighted 10 miles ahead. The *Greer* slowed down to allow her sonar operator to track the U-Boat, purely as a precaution, but one which was inevitably taken by the U-Boat to mean that the *Greer* was hunting her. For nearly four hours the destroyer tracked the U-Boat, during which time the British patrol plane dropped four depth-charges. Eventually the U-Boat commander, exasperated at what he regarded as highly 'un-neutral' tactics, fired a torpedo. To this the *Greer* replied by

Below: The elderly flush-decker HMS *Claire* was converted to a Long Range Escort by the replacement of two boilers with extra fuel tanks.

dropping depthcharges, but when it was clear that the U-Boat had escaped she continued on her way to Iceland. The outcome was that US warships were given clear instructions to defend shipping in the North Atlantic, the 'shoot on sight' order which permitted USN escorts to attack German or Italian submarines.

The next incident was more serious, for on 17 October the new destroyer *Kearny* (DD.432) was torpedoed by *U.568*. Once again the US destroyers were hopelessly mixed up with British, Canadian and even Free French escorts, all trying to cope with a Canadian convoy which had been heavily attacked by a wolf-pack. It was about 0200 and she had just dropped depth-charges (US destroyers were permitted to drop charges to 'embarrass' or frighten off U-Boats). In the intermittent glare from a burning tanker the U-Boat fired a spread of three torpedoes, and one of these caught the *Kearny* in the forward fire-room. There was a tremendous explosion, which tore up the deck and 11 men were killed and 24 wounded. The ship had been at battle stations, so the flooding could be contained as long as the forward fire-room bulkhead held up under strain.

The *Bensons* were the first destroyers built with machinery on the 'unit' system with turbines and boilers alternated to reduce the risk of the entire steam plant being knocked out by one hit, and the *Kearny*'s experience showed how important it was in enabling destroyers to withstand action damage. Certainly the unit system saved the *Kearny*, and she was able to limp to Iceland under her own power, escorted by the *Greer*. There she was secured alongside the repair ship *Vulcan* and patched up for the journey back to a proper repair yard.

The old four-stacker *Reuben James* (DD.245) was not so lucky. Exactly two weeks after the torpedoing of the *Kearny* she was escorting an eastbound convoy near the 'MOMP' or Mid-Ocean Meeting Point at which US destroyers handed over convoys to British and Canadian escorts. Just before dawn on 31 October

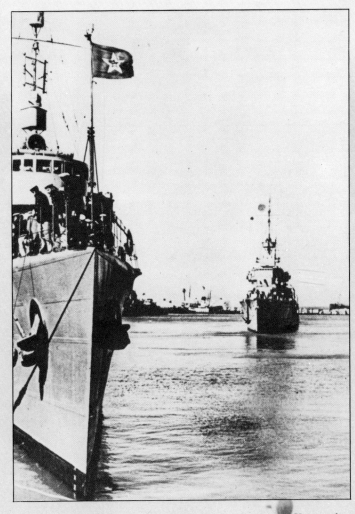

Above: Russian destroyers of the Baltic Fleet at the port of Kronstadt.

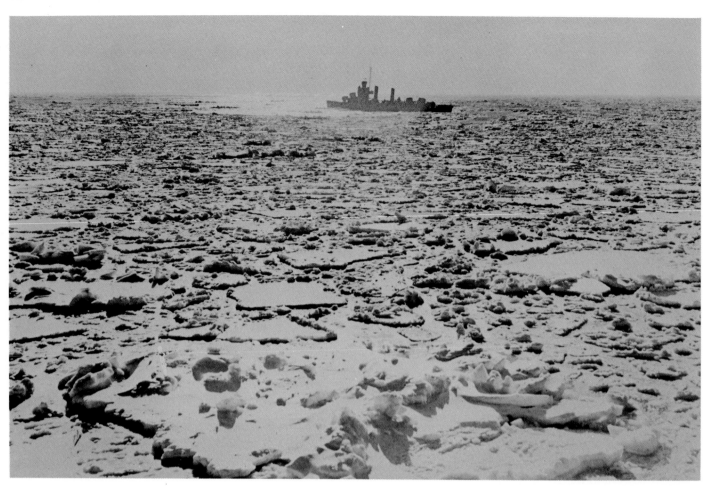

Above: USS *Gleanes* skirts the ice floes in the North Atlantic.

she was torpedoed on the port side and her entire fore-part disappeared in a massive explosion. Evidently the forward 4-inch magazine had detonated because all that was left of the *Reuben James* was the after-part from the fourth funnel to the stern. The shattered remnant of the hull stayed afloat for about five minutes, and as it sank the depth-charges exploded, killing many of the survivors. More than two-thirds of her complement including her captain, were killed or drowned, but even this was not enough to end isolationism in the United States. President Roosevelt immediately sought approval from Congress to transfer the Coast Guard to the control of the Navy and within two weeks further amendments to the Neutrality Act were passed but it was to take Pearl Harbor to convince the Americans that World War II had arrived.

Paradoxically, once the United States was at war with Germany the confrontation between US destroyers and U-Boats in the Atlantic diminished. The reason was simply that destroyers were desperately needed for the Pacific, and so it was agreed that the main contribution to the Battle of the Atlantic would be maritime aircraft for the RAF and destroyer escorts (DEs) for the Royal Navy.

The destroyers earmarked for Atlantic duties were more urgently needed to convoy troopships to the British Isles, but in August 1942 the *Emmons* and *Rodman* escorted the cruiser *Tuscaloosa* to North Russia. In September 1942 a South Atlantic Force of four old light cruisers and eight destroyers was created, to protect Brazilian shipping against U-Boats, and some of the old destroyers operated in the Caribbean to cope with the U-Boats' *Paukenschlag* ('Drumroll') offensive against American shipping.

In the last week of May 1941 the 4th Flotilla of the Home Fleet, comprising four Tribal Class, the *Cossack, Maori, Sikh* and *Zulu* and the Polish *Piorun* (ex-HMS *Nerissa*) was escorting a troop convoy when the news came that the German battleship *Bismarck* had broken out through the Denmark Strait, and had sunk the battlecruiser HMS *Hood* and shaken off the battleship *Prince of Wales* and two shadowing cruisers. On 26 May Captain Vian was ordered to join the Home Fleet, but when he intercepted a PBY Catalina's sighting report he altered course for the *Bismarck* on his own initiative, with the intention of slowing her down by torpedo attack.

Taking station on the cruiser *Sheffield*, which was in radar contact with the *Bismarck*, Vian led his destroyers through heavy seas to take up positions for a night attack. So bad were conditions that his own leader, HMS *Cossack*, and her next astern, the *Maori*, were swung right around at a speed of 26 knots. The two destroyers missed one another by a matter of feet and found that they had changed places in the line, but in the heat of the moment nobody paused to draw breath. At about 2200 the massive bulk of the *Bismarck* was sighted by the *Piorun*, silhouetted by the flash of her own guns. Vian wanted his destroyers to box her in before launching a coordinated attack, but the weather was so bad that even when easing down to 18 knots the lookouts were blinded by spray. There was no moon either, so Vian decided to allow his destroyers to attack independently. At ranges which varied from 6000 down to as little as 4000 yards the five destroyers dodged and weaved, while the tired gun-layers aboard the battleship tried to blast them out of the water. It was probably only their wild gyrations which saved the destroyers from being hit by anything bigger than splinters, but for all their efforts they could not hit the *Bismarck*. During the action the worried radar operator aboard the *Cossack* reported a number of shapes on his screen; it was realized that the air-warning radar had picked up the *Bismarck*'s 2000-pound shells in mid-flight.

At about 0300 the battered destroyers lost touch with the *Bismarck*. Although her radio aerials were shot away the *Cossack* had been able to broadcast a series of bearings to the

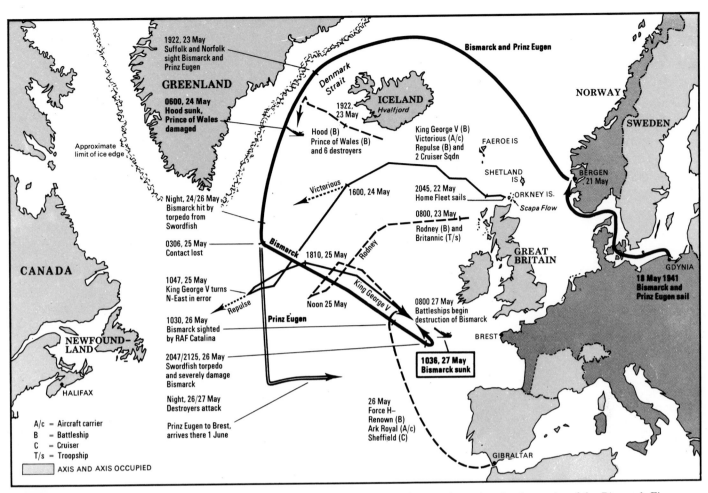

1922, 23 May
Suffolk and Norfolk
sight Bismarck and
Prinz Eugen

GREENLAND

0600, 24 May
Hood sunk,
Prince of Wales
damaged

Denmark Strait

Bismarck and Prinz Eugen

ICELAND
Hvalfjord

NORWAY

SWEDEN

1922,
23 May

Approximate
limit of ice edge

Hood (B)
Prince of Wales (B)
and 6 destroyers

King George V (B)
Victorious (A/c)
Repulse (B) and
2 Cruiser Sqdn

FAEROE IS

BERGEN
21 May

SHETLAND
IS

Victorious

1600, 24 May

2045, 22 May
Home Fleet sails

ORKNEY IS.
Scapa Flow

Night, 24/26 May
Bismarck hit by
torpedo from
Swordfish

0800, 23 May
Rodney (B) and
Britannic (T/s)

CANADA

0306, 25 May
Contact lost

Bismarck

1810, 25 May

Rodney

GREAT
BRITAIN

GDYNIA

18 May 1941
Bismarck and
Prinz Eugen sail

1047, 25 May
King George V turns
N-East in error

King George V

Repulse

Noon 25 May

0800 27 May
Battleships begin
destruction of Bismarck

NEWFOUND-
LAND

1030, 26 May
Bismarck sighted
by RAF Catalina

Prinz Eugen

BREST

2047/2125, 26 May
Swordfish torpedo
and severely damage
Bismarck

1036, 27 May
Bismarck sunk

HALIFAX

Night, 26/27 May
Destroyers attack

26 May
Force H–
Renown (B)
Ark Royal (A/c)
Sheffield (C)

A/c = Aircraft carrier
B = Battleship
C = Cruiser
T/s = Troopship

Prinz Eugen to Brest,
arrives there 1 June

GIBRALTAR

AXIS AND AXIS OCCUPIED

Above: The map shows the nine-day cruise of the *Bismarck*. Five destroyers under Captain Vian made a night attack on the mighty ship shortly before she was smashed by the battleships HMS *Rodney* and *King George V*.
Left: Impressive though it looks, the 4-inch forecastle gun of a destroyer would have been woefully ineffective against a capital ship.

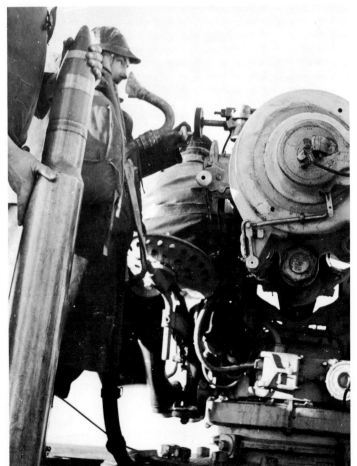

Commander in Chief, Home Fleet. Although a final attempt was made by the *Maori* and *Sikh* to attack at 0700, the battleships *King George V* and *Rodney* were in sight, and so Vian's destroyers hauled off and left it to the big ships to play out the final act of the drama. Although they had not damaged the *Bismarck* they had carried out the destroyer's traditional role of shadowing and harassing an enemy capital ship, and the constant alarms and expenditure of ammunition did nothing to improve her chances of surviving the fleet action next morning.

Destroyers also put paid to the career of the battlecruiser *Scharnhorst* in December 1943. The immediate cause of this had been Hitler's understandable anger when a force of eight British destroyers had fought off an attempt by the pocket-battleship *Lützow*, the heavy cruiser *Admiral Hipper* and destroyers to attack their convoy. This action, known as the Battle of the Barents Sea, was fought in December 1942. One of the destroyers fought a brilliant delaying action to give time for the distant escort of two cruisers to come up and drive away the *Lützow* and *Hipper*. It was at this point that the destroyer *Friedrich Eckholdt* closed with the cruisers *Jamaica* and *Sheffield* under the impression that they were friendly, only to be blasted with 6-inch shells.

Hitler was not prepared to allow the Allies to run convoys to North Russia or to deploy their heavy ships in other theaters, and so another operation against a convoy was planned in 1943. A proposal to use the big destroyers alone was amended to include the *Scharnhorst*, but the greatly superior British radar would count against the Germans during the long hours of Arctic night.

Admiral 'Achmed' Bey, the man who had turned the tables on Warburton-Lee's destroyers at the First Battle of Narvik in 1940, commanded Northern Group's destroyers, and he took over as Flag Officer Northern Task Force when Admiral Kummetz went on leave in November. When his flagship sailed from Alten Fjord at 1900 on Christmas Day he was not to know that all the assumptions made by his staff were wrong. There was not one convoy but two, JW.55B homeward bound for England, and RA.55A bound for Murmansk. Aerial reconnaissance had detected only JW.55B, covered by a close escort force of three cruisers and destroyers, and although the Home Fleet had been detected leaving Iceland, the Luftwaffe report had been vaguely worded. It mentioned the possibility of a battleship being included, but in accordance with the rule that only facts were to be passed on to the Navy, this afterthought was deleted. But there was a battleship, the 38,000-ton *Duke of York*, flagship of the Commander in Chief Home Fleet, Admiral Fraser. Fraser was very well-informed about the *Scharnhorst*'s intentions, almost undoubtedly as a result of Ultra cryptanalysis, and had already ordered four destroyers to transfer from the undetected convoy to JW.55B's close escort. Bey was moving into a trap, with a battleship, a cruiser and four destroyers moving up at high speed to cut off his retreat and a total of 14 destroyers actually with the convoy, in company with three modern cruisers.

As a destroyer man himself, Bey must have had misgivings when he allowed his own destroyers to turn back, but they could not keep station with the flagship in the worsening weather. The Luftwaffe reconnaissance aircraft were now grounded as well, and the *Scharnhorst* was without any information apart from what could be seen by her radar and the eyes of her lookouts. U-Boats had given him reasonable estimates of the size, speed and course of the convoy, but they failed to sight the Home Fleet. Fraser's signals to his scattered forces were concise, to minimize the risk of attacks on friendly forces, whereas the German destroyers lost contact with the *Scharnhorst* early on the morning of 26 December and there was no way to recall them.

At 0840 on 26 December the cruiser flagship *Belfast* picked up a large 'blip' on her radar screen, which indicated that the *Scharnhorst* was only 30 miles away. As the *Duke of York* was still 200 miles away, the cruisers had to fight a holding action, which they proceeded to do in masterly fashion. At 0924 starshells from the *Belfast* lit up the *Scharnhorst* in the predawn Arctic gloom, and in only two minutes one of HMS *Norfolk*'s 8-inch shells demolished the forward fire-control director and its radar antenna. The startled *Scharnhorst* sheered off, and in the heavy seas she soon pulled away from the three cruisers. Admiral Burnett was too wily to allow his cruisers to be drawn away from the convoy, and confidently forecast that the enemy would be back. Within three hours his prediction was proved correct when the *Scharnhorst* was sighted again, coming up from the south. This time she made a more determined effort

to push past the cruisers, and the range came down to 11,000 yards as her 11-inch shells bracketed them with accurate salvoes. The *Norfolk* was hit several times but the delay distracted the Germans' attention, and during the mêlée the *Duke of York* approached to within 12,000 yards without being seen.

There were four destroyers with the cruisers, the *Matchless*, *Musketeer*, *Opportune* and *Virago*, and they had already launched a torpedo attack to take the pressure off. The heavy seas made it very difficult to overhaul the *Scharnhorst*, and although all four destroyers got close enough to fire their puny 4.7-inch and 4-inch guns at the battlecruiser the range was too great for an effective torpedo attack.

The British battleship had plenty of time to maneuver and bring the maximum number of guns to bear, and at 0450 the first starshell burst over the *Scharnhorst*, followed immediately by salvoes of 14-inch and 6-inch shells. Once again the *Scharnhorst* tried to break away, but this time her opponent was able to keep up, for the heavy seas evened out any nominal differences between the two ships' top speeds. The cruisers were left behind as the big ships traded punches at a range of 17,000–20,000 yards.

A 14-inch hit damaged one of the *Scharnhorst*'s propeller shafts, and Admiral Fraser signalled to his four destroyers to attack with torpedoes.

It has already been mentioned that the weather was too rough for the German destroyers, and so bad that even 10,000-ton cruisers were unable to maintain full speed. The *Saumarez*, *Savage*, *Scorpion* and *Stord* (Norwegian Navy) displaced only 2000 tons fully loaded, and their frail hulls whipped and shuddered as they plunged through the waves and buried themselves in clouds of spray. The *Saumarez* and the *Savage* slowly drew away from the *Duke of York* and crept up on their quarry. The *Scorpion* and *Stord* worked their way on to the starboard quarter, leaving the other pair of destroyers to draw fire on the port side. The *Saumarez* and *Savage* came under heavy fire, but the *Scorpion* and *Stord* managed to approach to within 3000 yards, virtually point-blank for a torpedo attack. At least one of the *Scorpion*'s torpedoes hit, and the *Scharnhorst* turned away, straight into the arms of the other two destroyers. Once again shuddering underwater explosions told that three torpedoes had hit. The destroyers had done their job, and they eased down thankfully as the *Duke of York* took over the work of finishing the battle. The range was now only 10,400 yards and the cruisers were joining in, firing at the dull smoky glow that was all that anyone could make out in the murk. It was all over by 1945, when the cruisers closed in to find only 36 men out of the 2000 who had been aboard at Alten Fjord only a day before.

The Battle of the North Cape was the last major action in European waters and it marked the end of the Germany Navy's attempt to dominate the Atlantic. Undoubtedly the contribution of the destroyers in the battle was a most important part of the victory, for if they had not slowed the *Scharnhorst* down she could have eluded the Home Fleet and possibly have returned safely to base.

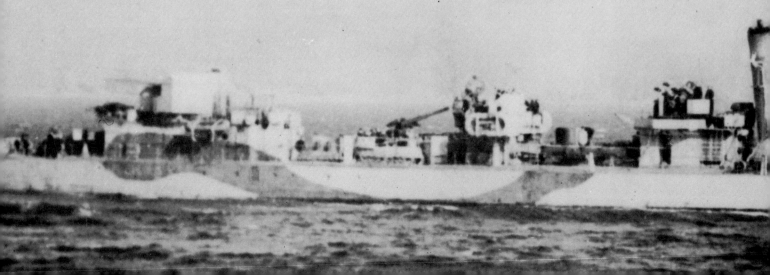

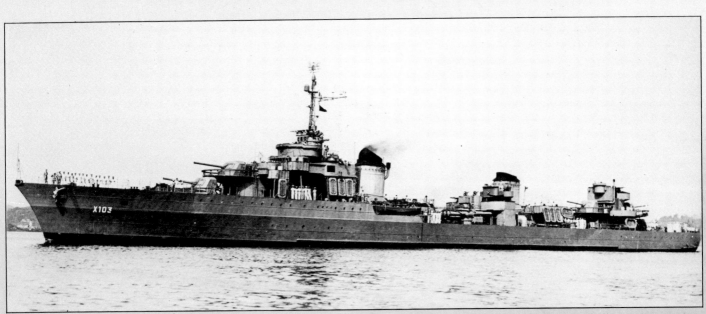

Above: The French destroyer *Le Fautargue* in 1940.
Right: HMS *Nepal* approaches HMS *Queen Elizabeth* as her seamen prepare to fire a line across. The destroyer was first named *Norseman* but was damaged by German bombs while building.
Below: Destroyers in service on the Arctic convoys were given special equipment to combat the intense cold. HMS *Musketeer* and others had steam-heated gun mountings and asbestos insulation for their bulkheads.

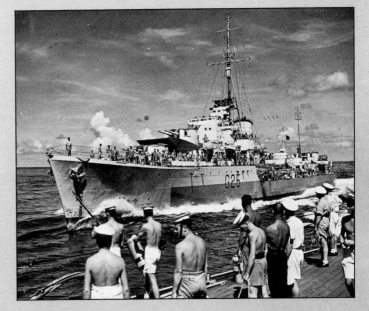

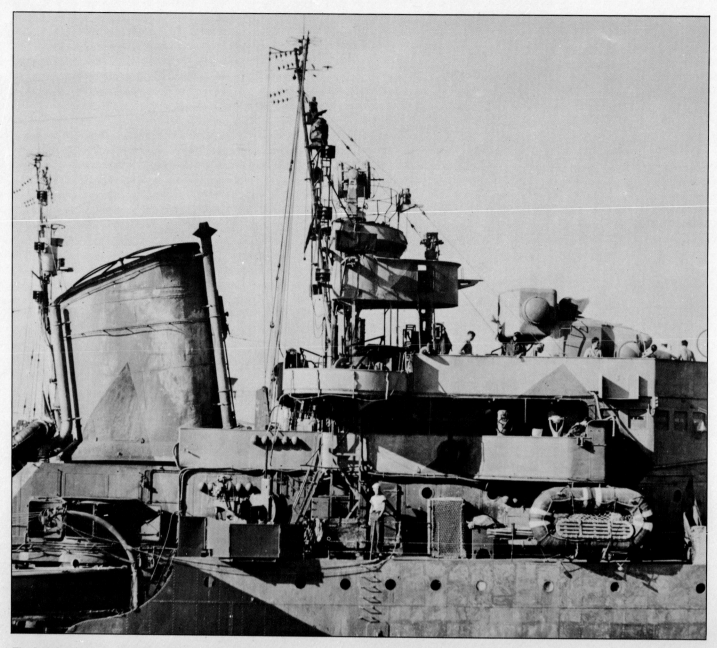

The Italian destroyer *Folgore* was sunk by the guns of Royal Navy cruisers and destroyers in December 1942.
Below: French and British warships at Alexandria in the early stages of the war.

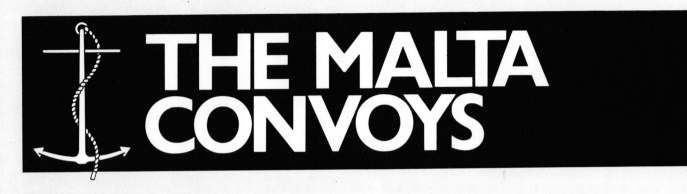

THE MALTA CONVOYS

Destroyers played an important part in Mediterranean naval operations partly because of the shorter distances but above all because the British destroyers were often the only vessels capable of matching the Italian warships' high speed.

The very first action of the Mediterranean, the action off Calabria on 9 July 1940, set a pattern which was to become familiar in the next three years. The Italian Fleet was sighted by the British cruisers at long range, and although a gunnery duel started, the Italians broke off when the flagship *Giulio Cesare* was hit by HMS *Warspite* at nearly 25,000 yards. Cunningham's destroyers, three flotillas totalling 14 boats, raced after the fleeing Italians but failed to make contact. The Italian destroyers did their work well, laying dense smoke-screens and engaging with gunfire, and by the time the British flotillas pushed past and penetrated the smoke-screens the Italian battleships were hull down on the horizon, heading for home.

The next action, off Cape Spartivento four months later, was even more disappointing, and the destroyers could not even get into action, but in March 1941 the third of these 'stern-chase' engagements turned into the decisive battle which Cunningham hankered after, the Battle of Cape Matapan.

The fortunes of war change very rapidly, and the triumph of Matapan was quickly followed by the Royal Navy's most gruelling test of the entire war, the Battle for Crete. Following rough handling of the Italian invaders by the Greek Army and its British allies, Hitler decided to retrieve Mussolini's fortunes by sending German troops into Yugoslavia on 6 April 1941. Within two weeks the British and Greek forces were overwhelmed and forced to withdraw to Crete. There they were virtually devoid of any air cover as the RAF had been pulled back to Egypt, and the defense of the island was left to the Mediterranean Fleet. The Royal Navy had two tasks: first, to prevent a seaborne invasion, and second, to cover the evacuation of as many of the garrison as possible. It succeeded in both of these aims, but at a terrible cost in lives and ships.

On 20 May 1941 the Luftwaffe began to attack the ships patrolling north of Crete in conjunction with landings of gliders and paratroops on the island. Next day the destroyer *Juno* was sunk southeast of Crete when a bomb from an Italian high-level bomber detonated her magazine; she sank in two minutes. That night Rear-Admiral Glennie, with the cruisers *Dido*, *Orion* and *Ajax* and the destroyers *Janus*, *Kimberley*, *Hasty* and *Hereward* found a convoy of light craft, including commandeered Greek fishing boats, crowded with German invasion troops. Here at last was a tangible enemy, and the cruisers and destroyers ran amok, firing indiscriminately at anything they could see. When they had finished two and one-half hours later the invasion convoy had ceased to exist, and an estimated 4000 German troops had been killed or drowned. A seaborne invasion of Crete was not possible so long as the sea passage was disputed.

Next day the air attacks began again with renewed ferocity. The destroyers were particularly vulnerable when unsupported by larger ships for their antiaircraft armament was painfully weak. First to go was the *Greyhound*, and although the cruisers, *Gloucester* and *Fiji* tried to protect her, they were very low on antiaircraft ammunition; as soon as their defensive fire slackened the Stukas closed in and sank them as well. The destroyers patrolled north of the island on the lookout for invasion forces, but in fact the Germans and Italians had given up trying to run another convoy. Under cover of darkness destroyers found time to evacuate the King of Greece and the British envoy to Greece, another of the responsibilities which tended to be given to destroyers.

On the morning of 23 May the already famous 5th Flotilla under Captain Lord Louis Mounbatten found itself without heavy support as the big ships had been prematurely withdrawn because it was feared that they were low on ammunition. It was about 0800, and the *Kelly* was leading the *Kashmir, Kipling, Kelvin* and *Jackal* back to Alexandria after attacking a force of troop-carrying caiques. Suddenly the drone of aero-engines heralded the arrival of the dreaded Stukas, two dozen of them. The *Kashmir* was hit and sank very quickly, for the flimsy hull of a destroyer was easily ruptured by the explosion of a heavy bomb. Then the *Kelly*, making 30 knots was hit as she put her helm hard over. She lurched to port, and still moving fast, slid over and lay bottom up for half an hour before disappearing.

The dazed survivors, covered in oil fuel, had to endure machine-gunning until the Stukas ran low on fuel and returned to base. The *Kelvin* and *Jackal* were ordered to make their escape to avoid further losses, but the *Kipling* bravely stayed behind for three hours, and managed to rescue 279 survivors. The risks she ran were terrible, but abandoning flotilla-mates was not part of the destroyer tradition. On the way back to Alexandria the *Kipling* had another 80 bombs dropped at her, and when still 70 miles from home she suffered the ultimate indignity: she ran out of fuel and had to be towed into Alexandria.

Once the German paratroops gained a sizeable bridgehead in Crete the island was doomed, and the call went out for the Navy to make an even greater effort than it had already, by evacuating the 32,000 men of the garrison. It was another Dunkirk but under much greater difficulties.

Destroyers and the fast minelayer *Abdiel* had already been running in with urgently needed ammunition and stores as even the fastest merchantmen found the trip suicidal. The problem with Crete was that the only good port for offloading stores or embarking was on the north side, the side most exposed to German air attack. On the night of 28–29 May Rear-Admiral Rawlings took the cruisers *Orion, Ajax* and *Dido* and six destroyers into Heraklion in an attempt to evacuate the defenders.

At first everything went well, and by 0320 the 4000 troops were safely embarked. Then the *Imperial*'s steering gear jammed, probably as a result of near-misses during the daylight passage to Crete. Admiral Rawlings dared not allow his force to be caught so close to the Luftwaffe's airfields at daybreak and so he ordered the *Hotspur* to take off her troops and sink her. With 900 men on board the *Hotspur* rejoined an hour later, but it was too late, and the sun was up when the eight warships headed southwards through the Kaso Strait at the eastern end of Crete. Soon they were picked up by Axis reconnaissance aircraft, and the bombing began at 0600. The *Hereward* was hit, but there was no question of turning back to help her; she drifted inshore before sinking, so fortunately the larger part of her crew and the soldiers she had embarked survived to become prisoners of war. The *Decoy* was also hit but managed to limp along at reduced speed. The *Dido* and *Orion* were hit by bombs, and a second attack two hours later killed or wounded over 500 troops packed in the *Orion*'s forward mess-decks.

While this was going on another four destroyers had managed to get 700 troops out of the tiny harbour of Sphakia on the southeast coast virtually without loss. The reason was that,

unlike Admiral Rawlings' force, the air cover planned had been in the right place at the right time. Encouraged, Cunningham decided to continue the evacuation, and the following night the cruisers *Phoebe, Perth* and *Calcutta*, the fast transport *Glengyle* and three destroyers rescued a further 6000 men from Sphakia without losing a ship. The destroyers made one last effort on the night of 31 May–1 June and saved 4000 men, bringing the total to over 18,000 landed safely in Egypt.

The fall of Crete left the British in a precarious position, with all the gains since July 1940 wiped out. Their only forward base, the island of Malta, was cut off and liable to be bombed or starved into submission. The defeat of the Eighth Army in Libya meant that the Italian Navy could run supply convoys into Benghazi and Tripoli out of reach of the surface and air forces. Malta was now unusable by surface forces and its airfields were only barely usable by its defending fighters. To add to the Navy's burdens, the fortress of Tobruk and the Eighth Army's advance bases on the Libyan frontier had to be supplied by sending ships along 'Bomb Alley', a route dotted with wrecks.

The need to keep Malta supplied required far greater exertions. As early as May 1941 the Admiralty had increased the number of submarines in the Mediterranean, first by ordering a flotilla based on Gibraltar to operate against Italian shipping in the Tyrrhenian Sea and then by allocating some of the newly constructed submarines to the flotilla based on Malta. Throughout the summer of 1941 these submarines played havoc with the Italian supply convoys, backed up by air attacks. In September two aircraft carriers, the *Ark Royal* and *Furious* ferried 49 Hurricane fighters as a prelude to flying in twin-engined bombers to reestablish a strike force on the island. The success of these moves led to the reestablishment of a surface strike force at Malta in October 1941.

Known as Force K, it comprised the light cruisers *Aurora* and *Penelope* and the destroyers *Lance* and *Lively*, under the command of Captain W G Agnew RN.

Force K had only one brief, to deny the Axis forces the sea route between Italy and North Africa, and it quickly showed how vulnerable that route was. On 8 November a reconnaissance aircraft reported a convoy, 40 miles east of Cape Spartivento, seven merchant ships escorted by six destroyers, with a support force of two heavy cruisers and four destroyers. Ignoring these odds Agnew took his two cruisers and two destroyers in at first light next day and annihilated the convoy. All the merchant ships were sunk as well as the destroyer *Fulmine*, without loss, and the *Libeccio* was later torpedoed by the submarine *Upholder* while trying to rescue survivors; the support force apparently took no action to avoid the catastrophe.

Below: Throughout his long life Lord Mountbatten always retained a special regard for HMS *Kelly*, the flotilla leader which he captained. She was sunk by a German dive bomber during the Battle of Crete in May 1941.
Right: Three Italian torpedo boats of two world wars: (left to right) *Tilfone* (1942), *Antonio Mosto* (1915) and *Augusto Riboty* (1917).

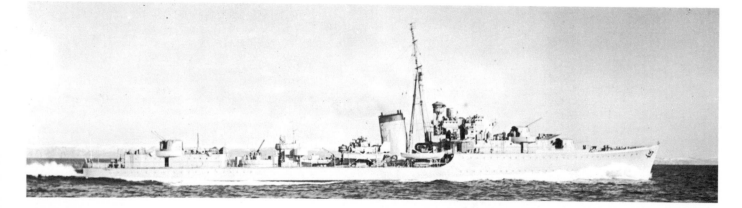

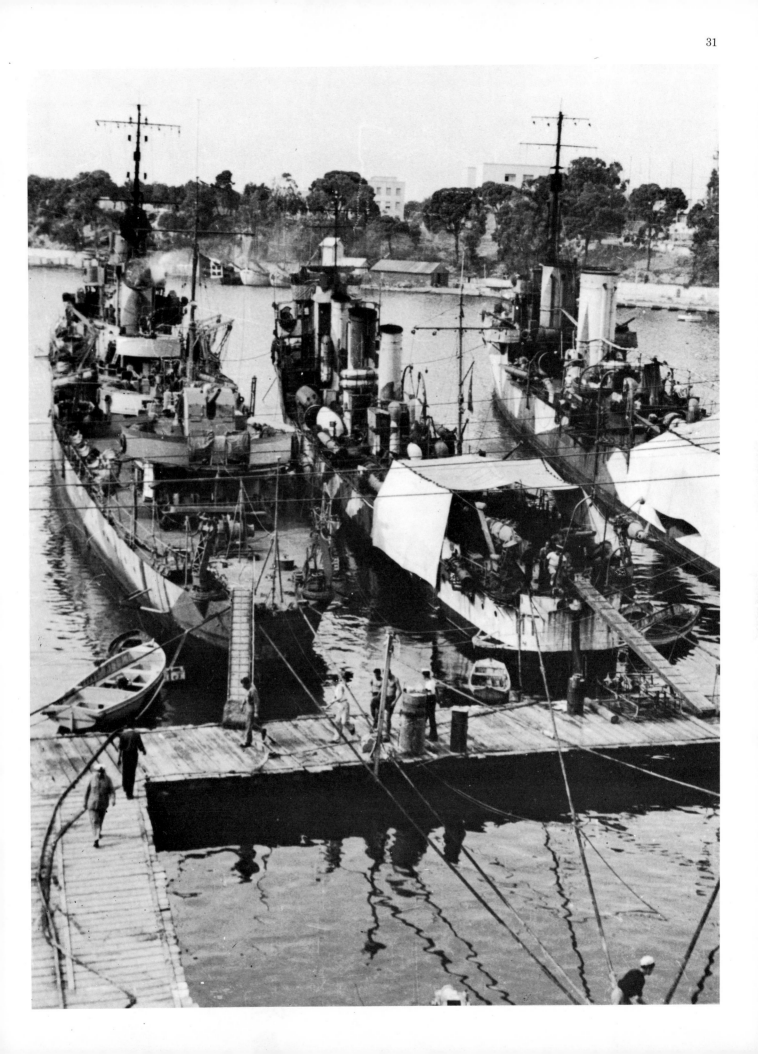

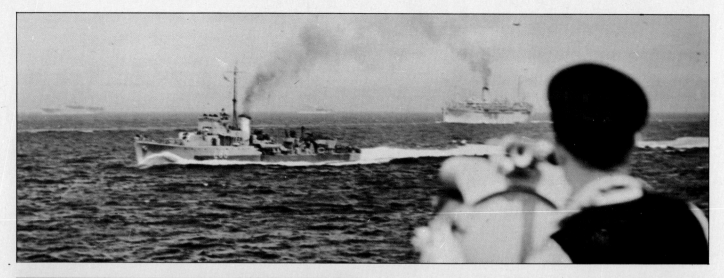

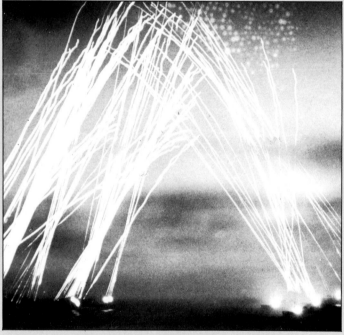

A week later the same four ships achieved another 100 percent success by wiping out a special convoy of two ships, the *Maritza* and *Procida*, carrying aviation gasoline urgently needed by the Luftwaffe in North Africa. The convoy was sighted 100 miles west of Crete, and despite a valiant defense by the two escorting torpedo boats, Force K sank the gasoline carriers with ease. On 29 November further reinforcements arrived at Malta, Force B under Rear-Admiral Rawlings, comprising the cruisers *Ajax* and *Neptune* and two more destroyers. Malta was an ulcer which threatened to drain the Axis strength in the Mediterranean, and for the first time the German command in North Africa began to talk of the possibility of defeat if Malta was not subdued. As if to underline this gloom, on 1 December Force K attacked and sank a supply ship and a tanker bound for Libya, as well as its escorting destroyer, the *Alvise da Mosto*.

On 13 December another action occurred, one of the most brilliant destroyer actions of World War II. This time there was no premeditation, for the *Sikh*, *Legion* and *Maori* and the Netherlands Navy's *Isaac Sweers* were merely en route from Gibraltar to Alexandria as reinforcements for Cunningham's

Top: Although suitable for the Mediterranean, French destroyers like *Le Fantasque* were unable to cope with severe Atlantic conditions.
Above: A massive concentration of antiaircraft fire protects the invasion fleet during Operation Torch against North Africa, November 1942.

14th Flotilla. So desperate had the fuel situation become in North Africa that the light cruisers *Alberico da Barbiano* and *Alberto di Guissano* had taken on a deck cargo of cased gasoline at Palermo, destined for Tripoli. When the sighting was made by a Wellington bomber from Malta it was intended that land-based torpedo-bombers and Force K would intercept, and the *Sikh* and her division were only meant to act in support, but at the last moment Force K was ordered to remain in Malta. Commander Stokes in HMS *Sikh* received fresh orders too late to reach the interception point, and to his chagrin he saw the two cruisers disappearing behind the high cliffs of Cape Bon. Stokes maintained course with little hope of catching the Italians, but suddenly he realized that the two cruisers had reversed their course and that he had an opportunity denied to most destroyer commanders for a set-piece attack against major warships.

What had happened was that the Italian squadron had been attacked by the RAF bombers without success, but Admiral Toscano expected to be attacked in much greater strength at daylight and had decided to turn back. Stokes led his destroyers close inshore so that they were hidden by the land behind them, with the Italians silhouetted against the skyline. At 0225 the *Sikh* fired a salvo of four torpedoes and saw the leading cruiser, the *Alberico da Barbiano* burst into flame as three of the 'fish' hit amidships. The *Legion* hit the *Alberto di Guissano* with only one torpedo, but she too burst into flame as gasoline drums on her decks burst and scattered flaming fuel everywhere. The *Maori* and *Isaac Sweers* pumped shells into the two hapless cruisers as they raced past. Only the second cruiser had time to fire three wild salvoes with her 6-inch guns, and seeing that their victims were beyond hope the four destroyers disappeared as quickly as they had arrived. The torpedo boat *Circe* picked up survivors, but a large number of lives were lost including the unlucky Admiral Toscano. His superiors at *Supermarina*, the Italian Naval HQ, had warned him of the presence of the four enemy destroyers but had considered that four destroyers would not dare to tackle two cruisers; he would have done better to take his chances with the RAF at daybreak, for British land-based bombers had a dismal record of failure against Axis warships.

In January 1941 the Eighth Army's fortunes improved, and with the airfields in Cyrenaica back in British hands Admiral Cunningham felt more optimistic about the Navy's chances of running a convoy through to Malta. In March he asked Admiral Vian to escort a small convoy of fast merchantmen from Alexandria to Malta.

It was a desperate mission for Malta was nearly on its knees, but Cunningham pointed out to Vian that the Italians had never yet attacked through a smoke screen.

The Second Battle of Sirte was one of the most dashing exploits in Vian's career. It showed that even without a battle-fleet behind them the Royal Navy's light forces were able to force the Italians to treat them with respect. The 'Fighting Fifteenth,' otherwise known as Vian's 15th Cruiser Squadron, left Alexandria early on the morning of 20 March 1942 with 15 destroyers escorting the fast transports *Breconshire*, *Clan Campbell*, *Pampas* and *Talabot*. Two days later Vian was told the unwelcome news that Italian heavy units had left Taranto. Later the cruiser *Penelope* and the destroyer *Legion* joined the convoy bringing the total number of cruisers up to five, including the elderly antiaircraft cruiser *Carlisle* which was not equipped for surface action. Throughout the morning Italian bombers made desultory attacks with torpedoes and bombs, but with no result. The midday meal was eaten at Action Stations, sandwiches and mugs of tea, when a float plane suddenly dropped a string of red flares ahead of the convoy. A float plane could only have come from a cruiser or a battleship and the markers were intended to guide an enemy squadron.

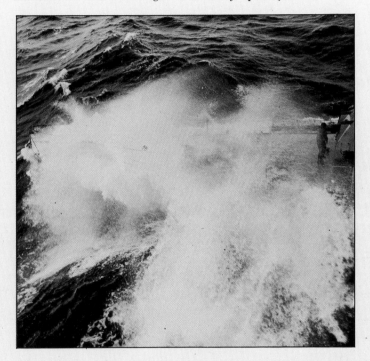

Above: Heavy seas crash over the bow of a destroyer.
Below: HMS *Kipling* and *Kimberley* of the 5th Flotilla. Eleven out of the 16 'J' and 'K' Class destroyers in the Mediterranean were lost.

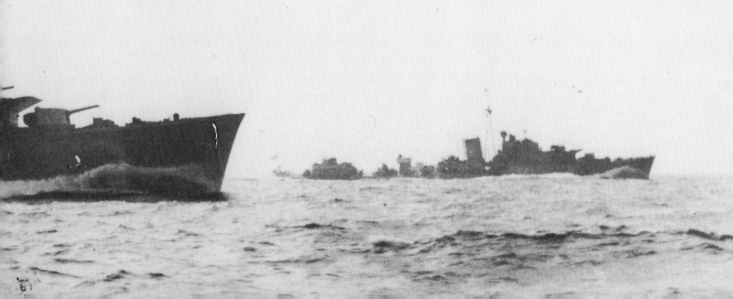

At 1410 the cruiser *Euryalus* reported smoke on the horizon and seven minutes later the masts and funnels of three big ships came into view. Vian signalled to the *Carlisle* and the six small 'Hunt' Class destroyers (which had no torpedo-tubes) to stay with the convoy and steer south towards Sirte to keep clear, while his flagship the *Cleopatra*, the *Dido*, *Euryalus* and *Penelope* and the fleet destroyers prepared to fight a surface action. 'Make smoke' was the order, and soon clouds of black funnel smoke and choking white clouds from the chemical smoke-floats mixed to form a screen between the Italian Fleet and the convoy. At 1436 two heavy cruisers and a light cruiser, afterwards identified as the *Gorizia, Trento* and *Giovanni delle Bande Nere*, opened fire on the 15th Cruiser Squadron at a range of 27,000 yards, but their shells fell short. The British cruisers were also out-ranged, but at a combined approach speed of 50 knots it was only a matter of minutes before the 5.25-inch guns of the *Cleopatra, Dido* and *Euryalus* were firing back. The rising wind made shell-spotting almost impossible for both sides and no hits were scored. After an hour the Italian cruisers sheered off to the north but no sooner had Vian's cruisers regained contact with the convoy than the alarm bells sounded again. The destroyer *Zulu* had sighted the enemy again, this time in two groups, the cruisers in one and the battleship *Littorio* 15 miles away with four destroyers.

For two hours the British cruisers and the destroyers played a lethal game with the Italians, daring them to come through the smoke-screen to face a torpedo attack. When the Italians tried to work their way around the westward end of the smoke-screen Vian used his destroyers to push them back. Hits were scored on both sides, but no serious damage was done as the ships weaved in and out of the smoke-screen in clouds of spray. Captain Poland and the 14th Flotilla made a determined torpedo attack on the enemy and forced him to withdraw. All this time sporadic bombing was taking place, an added distraction. It was 1820 before the Italians finally gave up and withdrew for the last time leaving the British to cope with what was now a mounting storm. In fact both sides suffered considerably more damage from the storm than from the gunfire; the *Littorio* returned to harbor with thousands of tons of water aboard and the destroyers *Lanciere* and *Scirocco* foundered that night. Vian's cruisers had to reduce speed to 18 knots and later to 15 knots; even then the destroyers fell behind and the *Zulu* had her forecastle stove in by a heavy sea.

Below: American destroyers began to operate in the Mediterranean with the Torch landings in November 1942. Seen here is USS *Swanson* (DD.443).

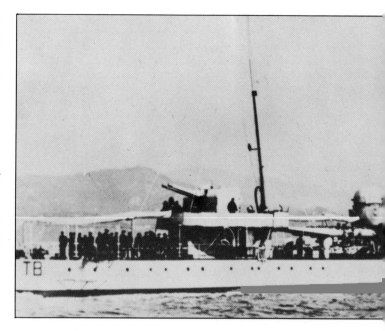

The last great Malta convoy was Operation Pedestal in August 1942 which called for the support of two battleships, three fleet carriers, seven cruisers and 20 destroyers to get only 14 fast cargo ships through. In a four-day battle nine merchantmen, a carrier and two cruisers were sunk, and a carrier and two cruisers were badly damaged. But Malta was saved particularly by the tanker *Ohio*, whose cargo of aviation gasoline was the most vital of all, for it was needed to keep the Spitfires and Hurricanes flying. The *Ohio* was crippled and had been on fire, but the destroyers *Penn* and *Ledbury* lashed themselves alongside to keep her afloat long enough to crawl into Bighi Bay. Although she sank at her moorings her cargo was intact, and it enabled Malta's aircraft to begin strikes against Rommel's supply convoys once more.

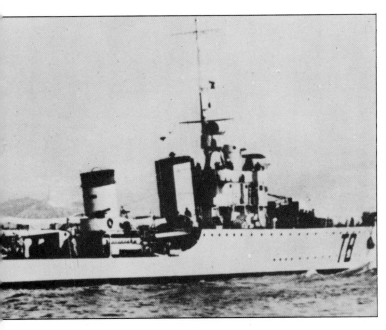

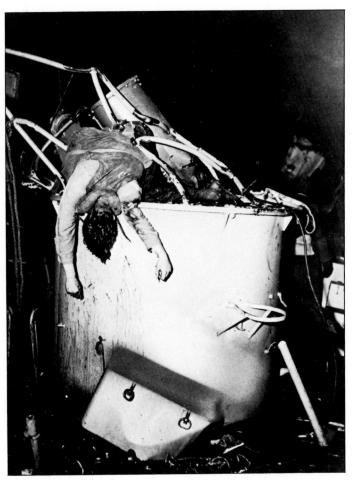

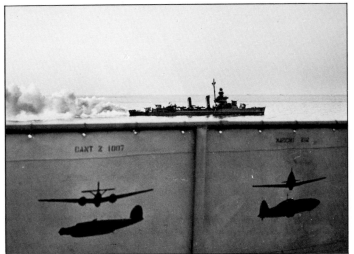

Top left: Italian destroyers suffered heavily at the hands of the Royal Navy. The *Turbine* was one of the casualties.
Left: A US destroyer lays a chemical smoke screen off the Salerno invasion beach. Aircraft identification silhouettes are painted on the rail.
Above: A dead US Coast Guardsman on the USS *Menges* (DE.320). The *Menges* was torpedoed by *U.371* in the western Mediterranean in 1944.

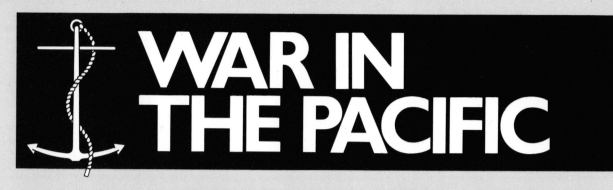

WAR IN THE PACIFIC

It was a destroyer of the US Pacific Fleet which had the first brush with the Japanese in World War II. The four-stacker *Ward* was on routine patrol off Pearl Harbor and in the early morning of 7 December she was heading for home after an uneventful two days. At 0357 she was warned by a minesweeper that something resembling the periscope of a submarine had been sighted. A sonar search revealed nothing, but about two and a half hours after the report the *Ward*'s lookouts spotted a small submarine trailing the target ship *Antares* on her way to the main entrance.

The old destroyer's crew was efficient, and the second 4-inch shell was seen to hit at a distance of less than a hundred yards. A pattern of depth-charges completed the destruction of the mystery submarine, which was in fact one of a force of midgets which had been launched from Japanese fleet submarines some distance away. The idea was that the attack was to coincide with the air strike which was already winging its way from Admiral Nagumo's carriers, and to profit by the resulting confusion in the anchorage. The subsequent failure to take note of the *Ward*'s timely action was just one more of the oversights and miscalculations which contributed to the disaster of Pearl Harbor.

After the Pearl Harbor raid destroyers were soon fighting in the East Indies. The US Asiatic Fleet had only 13 destroyers, all well past their prime, to defend the Philippines. When their base at Cavite was put out of action by Japanese bombers three days after Pearl Harbor, the Commander in Chief, Admiral Thomas C Hart had even less chance of protecting such an enormous area. Hart was ordered to get his destroyers to the Dutch East Indies, where in conjunction with Australian, British and Dutch warships, there might be some hope of defending the so-called 'Malay Barrier.'

Below: The Japanese captured USS *Stewart* at Surabaya in March 1942. They converted her to a fast fuel carrier, radically altering her appearance.

On 20 January 1942 the cruisers *Boise* and *Marblehead* and six destroyers of DesDiv 59 were ordered to attack a Japanese force of transports heading for Balikpapan in eastern Borneo. The cruiser *Boise* damaged herself by hitting a pinnacle of rock and had to return to base escorted by a destroyer. Then the *Marblehead* developed machinery trouble and returned taking another destroyer as escort. This left only the elderly *John D Ford*, *Parrott*, *Paul Jones* and *Pope* to deal with an amphibious force escorted by the light cruiser *Naka* and 12 destroyers. But fortune favors the bold, and Commander Talbot's tiny force reached Balikpapan undetected; the Dutch had set the oil refinery on fire and huge clouds of smoke shrouded the anchorage. It was ideal for a destroyer attack, with the transports at anchor in the harbor silhouetted against the glow of fires ashore.

The destroyers raced in aiming their first torpedoes at a line of transports outside the harbor. The *Parrott* fired three torpedoes but obtained no hit, and then launched another salvo of five, but it also missed. Two more torpedoes fired by the *John D Ford* and *Paul Jones* also missed, although the range was down to 1000 yards.

The Japanese were now alert to the fact that an attack was in progress and the anchorage soon bustled with activity as alarm bells sounded and guns fired. Fortunately for the Americans the Japanese destroyers seem to have been ordered to start a submarine hunt and the ships remained undetected for a while longer. During a second attack three of the *Parrott*'s 'fish' behaved properly, and this time a transport blew up. The column of destroyers left a trail of destruction as they ran southwards sinking another transport and a patrol craft totalling 23,000 tons of shipping. When they had no torpedoes left they used their 4-inch guns to sink another transport before leaving the scene. The confusion and destruction they had caused was out of all proportion to their relative strength for all four were 'four-stackers' built in World War I, and officially regarded as unfit for front-line service.

It was the only success scored by ABDA. The Japanese continued their inexorable drive on the East Indies, investing Singapore in the west and reaching as far as Rabaul in the east. With the flanks in enemy hands the center was soon untenable; Surabaya on the north side of Java was threatened, and Tjilatjap on the south side was the only other suitable base. A holding action was needed, and so the Dutch Admiral Karel Doorman

was given command of a Combined Allied Striking Force, comprising the US cruisers *Houston* and *Marblehead*, the Dutch cruisers *de Ruyter* (flagship) and *Tromp*, the US destroyers *Barker*, *Bulmer*, *John D Edwards* and *Stewart* and the Dutch destroyers *Banckert*, *Piet Hein* and *Van Ghent*. To avoid the risk of air attack Doorman proposed a night attack on the Japanese invasion forces in the Makassar Strait but, to be in position by nightfall the task force had to cross the Java Sea in daylight.

Inevitably the Combined Striking Force was sighted by Japanese aircraft and a force of bombers attacked in the morning of 4 February. The cruisers were the main target and when both the *Houston* and *Marblehead* were badly hit Admiral Doorman ordered a return to Tjilatjap. With reinforcements from Surabaya, the British cruiser *Exeter*, the Australian *Hobart*, the Dutch *Java* and three more Dutch and US destroyers, Doorman was ordered to launch another strike to protect Palembang, the capital of Sumatra. This raid on 15 February suffered six hours of bombing and again Doorman had to order his ships to retire; as the British had learned in the Mediterranean, naval operations could not be mounted without air cover. The surrender of Singapore, announced the same day, marked the beginning of the end. Admiral Hart was recalled to the United States. His successor was the Dutch Admiral Conrad Helfrich.

Attrition was taking its toll of ABDA's destroyers; the Dutch

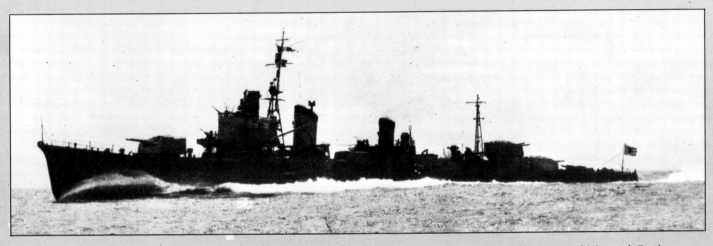

Above: The Japanese destroyer *Hayanami* at high speed. On the measured mile at Kyogasaki in 1943 she attained a speed of 35.15 knots.

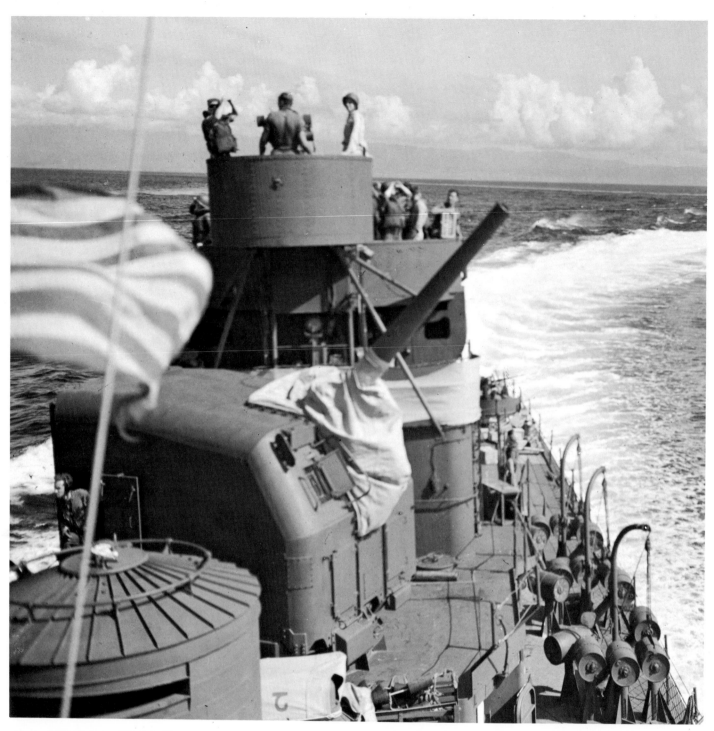

Above: USS *Nicholas* (DD.449). Her armament includes depth charges, torpedoes and 5-inch guns.

Van Ghent and *Kortenaer* both ran aground, while the USS *Peary* was sunk in a devastating Japanese bombing raid on Darwin in North Australia. The *Edsall* was damaged by a premature explosion of one of her depth-charges and the *Whipple* collided with the cruiser *de Ruyter*. The third attempt to halt the Japanese, a raid in the Badoeng Strait on 19 February, at last produced some results.

Some damage was caused to Japanese destroyers but in return the Dutch destroyer *Piet Hein* was sunk and the USS *Stewart* and the cruiser *Tromp* were disabled. The US destroyers were beginning to suffer from wear and tear as well as battle damage; operating so far from a main base meant that their tender, the *Black Hawk*, was running out of spares. Even under

ideal conditions a squadron of 'cans' needed constant nursing, and these destroyers had been afloat for a quarter of a century. By 20 February the ABDA force was reduced to five cruisers and nine destroyers, including three British, which had escaped from Singapore.

On 27 February Doorman's weary forces finally ran into the heavy ships which had been supporting the Japanese invasion, and the last round began. They were part of Admiral Kondo's Southern Striking Force, the heavy cruisers *Haguro* and *Nachi* and two groups of seven destroyers each, led by two outstanding Japanese destroyer leaders, Rear-Admirals Tanaka and Nishimura. Although on paper they did not have a big margin of strength over the ABDA Striking Force the Japanese had the priceless advantage of air cover, and their modern destroyers had the deadly 'Long Lance' 24-inch torpedo.

When the Japanese ships were sighted just after 1600 the the Allied force was steaming north, with the three British destroyers spread out in line abreast as a screen ahead of the line of cruisers, and the Dutch and American destroyers steaming in line ahead, parallel and on the port quarter. As the Japanese were steaming roughly southwest across their bows, this disposition meant that the bulk of Doorman's destroyers were on the disengaged side. It was the worst place to be, too far away to fire torpedoes, and as inter-Allied communications at this early stage of the war were poor, the destroyers were relying on garbled orders. At 1616 the Japanese opened fire from about 28,000 yards, bracketing the main column with accurate salvoes, and the cruiser *Jintsu* closed in to 18,000 yards to fire at the three destroyers leading the line. Doorman ordered his line to wheel to the west to avoid having his 'T' crossed, and as a result the destroyers were now level with the flagship *de Ruyter*.

The first casualty was the heavy cruiser HMS *Exeter*, which suffered a severe explosion on board. While the line was weaving to avoid her as she slowed down, a torpedo hit the *Kortenaer*. As a column of steam and smoke billowed up she seemed to pause for a moment, then turned turtle and broke in two. There was no time to look for survivors and the other destroyers hurried on, jockeying desperately for a position from which they could attack with torpedoes. The British destroyers tried to drive off the *Jintsu* but *Electra* was hit by a salvo of shells which left her sinking. The other two fell back to give assistance to the crippled *Exeter*, but the American destroyers were now in a position to attack, and in spite of a last-minute cancellation of the order, they carried out an attempt. Unfortunately the range was 10,000 yards, for anything closer would have been suicidal and all the torpedoes missed.

The cruisers had now disappeared, and the four destroyers tried to catch up. They eventually returned to Surabaya to refuel leaving Doorman and his cruisers to sail on to a further disastrous night action. Harassed by torpedo attacks in the light of flares dropped by Japanese float planes, the cruisers steamed on. At 2125 the *Jupiter* was suddenly blown up, and as no Japanese ships could be seen it was assumed that she had been mined, but it was just an example of the staggering range of the 'Long Lance' torpedo. By midnight the ABDA force was all but annihilated, with the *de Ruyter* and *Java* sunk and the *Houston* and *Exeter* badly damaged. The three surviving cruisers and two destroyers made their way back to Surabaya with nothing to show for their sacrifice. There was now nothing to

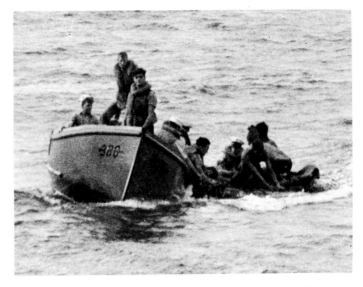

Above: USS *Helm*'s whaler picks up survivors from the oiler *Neosho* during the Battle of the Coral Sea.

stop the Japanese from capturing the entire East Indies. The following evening the cruisers *Houston* and *Perth* were sunk while trying to escape southwards through the Sunda Strait. On the morning of 1 March the *Exeter* and the destroyers HMS *Encounter* and USS *Pope* were trapped by the *Haguro* and *Nachi* in the Java Sea supported by two heavy cruisers.

The *Exeter* went down fighting, and when it was hopeless she ordered the two destroyers to make their escape while there was still time. The *Encounter* was hit by shellfire just after a destroyer torpedo finished off the *Exeter*, but the *Pope* managed to dodge behind a rain squall which hid her from the Japanese ships. With a faint chance of survival the old destroyer hurried away, making for the coast of Borneo, but suddenly the rain squall blew over, leaving her exposed once again. There were no ships in sight but a float plane from one of the cruisers spotted her

Below: USS *Conway*'s stern dips low in the water as she surges forward under full power.

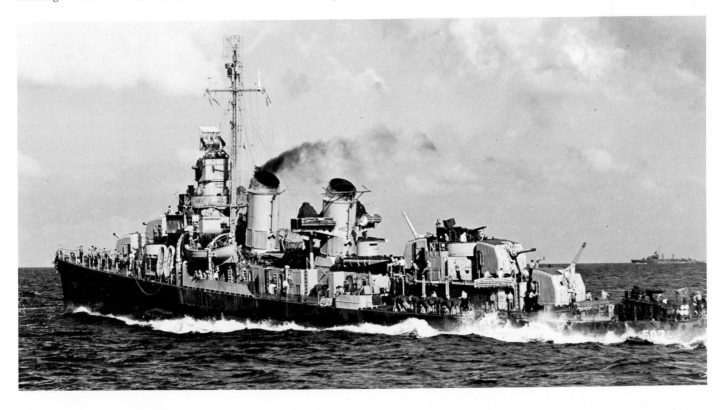

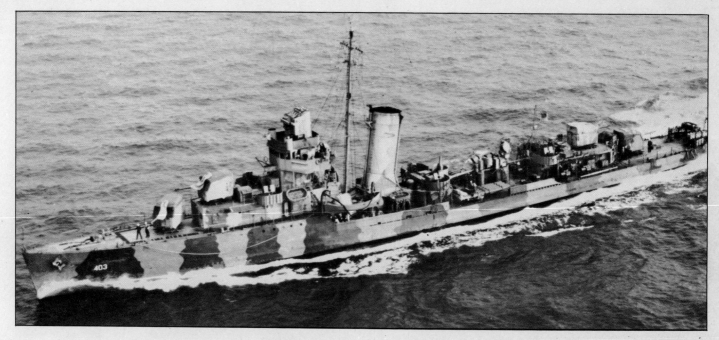

Above: USS *Trippe* (DD.403) underwent a refit in 1943. Half her torpedo tubes were removed to reduce weight above the waterline.

and within half an hour six dive bombers from the carrier *Ryujo* were on the scene. Incredibly, the *Pope* survived 13 attacks, and the carriers had to send a second group of bombers to finish her off.

On 7 August 1942, the US Marines landed on Guadalcanal in the Solomon Islands and seized an airstrip which had just been completed. They were not to know, as they triumphantly christened it Henderson Field, that they were witnessing the start of the most bitterly contested naval action of the entire Pacific War. Operation Watchtower had been launched to forestall the Japanese attempt to establish a foothold in the Solomons as a prelude to an attack on Australia. The Battle of the Coral Sea had checkmated an attempt to do it by seapower alone, but this time the Japanese intended to use all three services. The Americans were equally determined to stop them, for whoever possessed the Solomons chain held the key to the southwestern Pacific.

Below: The gallant carrier USS *Yorktown* lies stricken in the water during the Battle of Midway. A *Porter* Class destroyer stands by to give help.

The first day of the landings went reasonably well, with no opposition from the Japanese Navy, although heavy air attacks were mounted the next day. Not until the night of 8 August was it apparent what sort of nightmare was unfolding. USAAF bombers and a submarine reported seeing a force of Japanese warships leaving Rabaul. A series of delays prevented the reports from being dealt with, and the results were tragic. The force comprised five heavy and two light cruisers under Admiral Mikawa, and it was steaming at high speed towards the 'Slot,' otherwise known as Savo Sound, between Guadalcanal and the northern islands of the Solomons chain. Mikawa's cruisers were going to drive their way through the American and Australian warships to clear a path for six transports carrying reinforcements for the defenders of Guadalcanal.

The first mistake occurred on the morning of 9 August when Australian aircraft twice sighted Mikawa off Bougainville but delayed reporting it until late in the afternoon. The message had to go via Brisbane before it reached Admiral Victor Crutchley RN, whose three cruisers and two destroyers were on patrol in Savo Sound, and via Pearl Harbor before it reached Admiral Turner USN, in command at Guadalcanal. It was over eight hours before either flag officer received the report of the first sighting. The report included an erroneous sighting of 'seaplane tenders,' which led Admiral Turner to assume that an air attack rather than a gun and torpedo attack was most likely and once this idea had taken hold, other incorrect assumptions followed. Aerial reconnaissance might have cleared up the misunderstanding, but the US carriers had been withdrawn the night before to refuel, and bad weather had grounded the land-based search aircraft. At midnight the old submarine *S.38*, the same one which had first seen Mikawa's departure from Rabaul, torpedoed one of the six transports following the Japanese cruiser force. The remaining five turned back to Rabaul, but Mikawa's ships were now only 35 miles from Savo Island, still unsuspected.

The destroyer *Ralph Talbot* raised the alarm when one of the

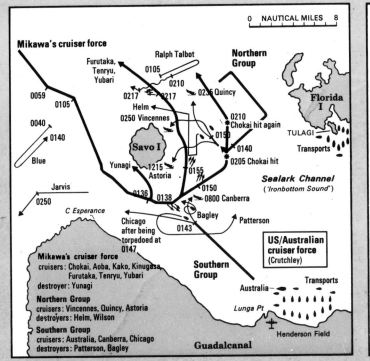

The Battle of Savo Island, 8 August 1942.

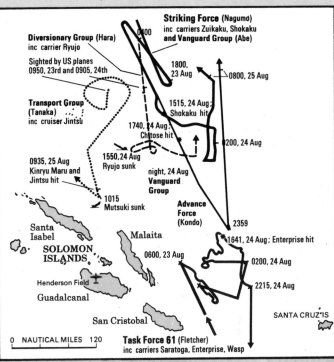

The Battle of the Eastern Solomons, 24 August 1942.

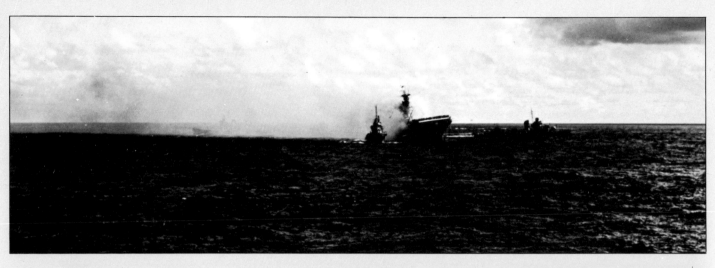

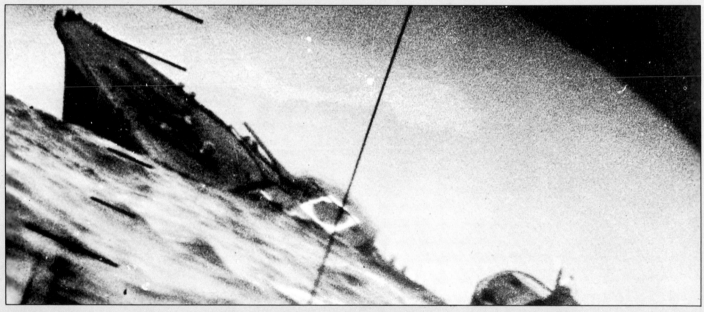

Top: The carrier USS *Hornet* was crippled by Japanese dive bombers at the Battle of Santa Cruz. To prevent the possibility of her capture by the enemy the destroyer USS *Mustin* put six torpedoes into her. However they failed to sink her and she was eventually sent to the bottom by Japanese torpedoes.

Above: The view through the periscope of USS *Nautilus* (SS.168) shows the Japanese destroyer *Yamakaze* slipping beneath the waves.

Japanese cruisers' float planes flew overhead, but bad radio reception prevented the call from getting through; her sister *Blue* picked it up and also made radar contact, but she also failed to make contact with Admiral Turner's flagship. In the sultry night, with changing visibility and rain squalls, the Japanese cruisers even managed to pass the *Blue* and *Ralph Talbot* without being detected. Both 'cans' were steaming away from the Japanese cruisers, and the lookouts were gazing ahead only, relying on the SC radar to give all-round surveillance. They were not to know that the mass of Savo Island nearby was producing a false echo which masked the echoes from the ships slipping past little more than 500 yards from the *Blue*. The next destroyer was the *Jarvis*, which had been torpedoed by a wave of torpedo bombers the day before; even if she had sighted the line of cruisers steaming at 25 knots her radio had been put out of action and there was no way in which to pass on a warning.

At 0143 the destroyer *Patterson* radioed an alarm, but it was too late. The float planes overhead dropped parachute flares to illuminate the Allied ships and a hail of gunfire and torpedoes was unleashed. The Australian cruiser *Canberra* was hit by 8-inch shells and then two torpedoes hit her on the starboard side.

She was soon on fire and completely disabled, but the *Patterson* was able to make some sort of reply. The *Bagley*, on the *Canberra*'s starboard bow, managed to get off a salvo of torpedoes, but too late. At 0147 a torpedo blew off the heavy cruiser *Chicago*'s bow, and she sheered off to the west away from the battle. The Japanese cruisers now moved north, splitting into two groups, and between Savo and Florida Island they fell in with the Northern Force, the heavy cruisers *Astoria*, *Quincy* and *Vincennes* with two destroyers. Like the Southern Force, which no longer existed, Captain Riefkohl's ships had been at action stations for up to 36 hours, and they had been allowed to stand down to the second state of readiness, with half the crew on watch and the other half turned in. The gun flashes to the south had been mistaken for the *Chicago* firing at aircraft, understandable in the light of the general assumption that an air attack was likely, and the *Chicago* had not sent any warning about surface ships. The three cruisers were in line ahead on a 'box patrol' at 10 knots, and were just turning on the northwest leg of the 'box' when they were sighted by Mikawa's flagship *Chokai*. The five American ships were in the worst possible position caught between the two Japanese columns.

The cruisers *Chokai* and *Aoba* opened fire quickly and scored hits on the *Quincy* before turning to the *Astoria* and *Vincennes*. The two destroyers were ignored, for the cruisers were after their own kind. In any case the *Helm* and *Wilson* were so confused that they achieved nothing apart from firing a few 5-inch shells. The *Ralph Talbot*, whose sighting of the float plane three hours earlier had failed to get through, was now punished by the light cruiser *Yubari* on the way out again. None of her torpedoes hit, and in return she was hit by several 140-mm shells. All power was lost, but before she could be sunk she was hidden by a rain squall, and managed to extinguish her fires and limp into Tulagi.

It was left to the destroyers to pick up the pieces. First there was the blazing hulk of the *Canberra*, and the *Patterson* risked

Below: *Akebono* and *Ushio* maneuver in line ahead.

exploding ammunition to go alongside and fight the fires. The *Blue* also came alongside and took off nearly 700 Australian survivors, and at 0800 the wreck was torpedoed by the *Ellett*.

The *Bagley* and *Helm* had already performed the same melancholy duty for the *Quincy* and *Vincennes* which had capsized about an hour after the action. The *Bagley* also rescued survivors of the *Astoria* and put a large firefighting party back on board to try and save her. With the *Wilson* she stood by all night until relieved by the *Buchanan*, but the efforts of all three destroyers were not enough and the crippled cruiser sank at midday. With four cruisers sunk and over 2000 men dead and injured, the Battle of Savo Island was a disaster for the Allies, and it showed that the lesson of Jutland had not been learned; one side had practiced night-fighting and the other side had not. The only crumbs of comfort were that Admiral Mikawa had failed to sink the transports lying off Lunga Point, and that on the way home the heavy cruiser *Kako* was torpedoed and sunk by the US submarine *S.44*. The men who lived through that night of destruction gave Savo Sound a new name to commemorate the ships which sank, Ironbottom Sound.

The Japanese Commander-in-Chief, Admiral Isoroku Yamamoto, was disappointed at the result of Savo Island battle, for the brilliant success of Mikawa in rolling up the Allied patrol line had not been followed by the destruction of the invasion force. During the inevitable lull which followed, the Japanese at Rabaul had been able to reinforce their garrisons on Guadalcanal and Tulagi. The ships which covered these supply runs also bombarded the Marines' positions ashore and threatened their supply lines. The chance was taken to build up a strong force for the task of expelling the Americans from the Solomons, with reinforcements from Truk and elsewhere. An Occupation Force of four transports with a close escort of four old destroyers and a cruiser was supported by a Mobile Force composed of the carriers *Ryujo*, *Shokaku* and *Zuikaku*, the seaplane carrier *Chitose*, three battleships, 11 cruisers and 23 destroyers. Against this the Allies had three carriers, the *Saratoga*, *Enterprise* and

Wasp, with one battleship, seven cruisers and 18 destroyers, split into three task forces.

The Battle of the Eastern Solomons on 24 August was another carrier battle in which the destroyers had little to do but act as handmaidens to the carriers. It was indecisive, as the American carriers' planes sank the carrier *Ryujo* in exchange for serious damage to the *Enterprise*. An interesting feature of the Japanese side of the operation was the use of four old destroyers of the *Mutsuki* Class, built in 1923–27, as fast transports. Their top sea speed was about 30 knots, and so they could keep up with a naval force unlike any ex-mercantile transport, and this made them useful for the high-speed runs from Rabaul to the Solomons. These runs were made with such monotony from August 1942 onwards that they were known to the Allies as the 'Tokyo Express.' On the morning of 25 August the *Mutsuki* was standing by the damaged transport *Kinryu Maru* when Army B-17s from Espiritu Santo scored a hit on her with bombs, which sank her. She was the first victim of USAAF medium-level bombs, and when Commander Hatano of the *Mutsuki* was rescued by the destroyer *Yayoi* it was reported that he said with a wry smile that it only proved that even the B-17s made a hit once in a while.

Japanese submarines were also present in the Solomons in growing numbers, and in the weeks after the Battle of the Eastern Solomons they showed how they could influence the campaign. On 31 August the carrier *Saratoga* was hit twice by torpedoes from *I.26*; although she was in the care of seven destroyers the force was zigzagging at only 13 knots to conserve the cans' fuel. The 'Sara' had been hazarded in a misguided attempt to provide cover for the fast convoys bringing supplies to Guadalcanal and Tulagi, and it was the same misuse of a fleet carrier which had caused the loss of HMS *Courageous* in September 1939. The American carrier was luckier, for she survived, but two weeks later on 14 September, three torpedoes from *I.19* ripped into the starboard side of the *Wasp*. This time the carrier was fatally damaged, and as her aviation gasoline burned it set off explosions of torpedoes and bombs, which made the job of the damage-control parties almost impossible. A sister of the *I.19*, the *I.15* was on station seven miles away, and she fired a spread of six torpedoes, one of which hit the battleship *North Carolina* abreast of A 16-inch gun turret, while a second ran on

Below: Destroyers of DesRon 12 make 'S'-turns in Ironbottom Sound to honor the dead. Savo Island is in the background.

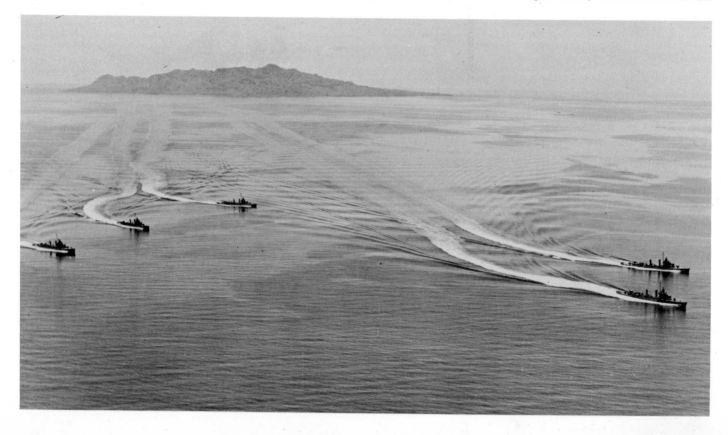

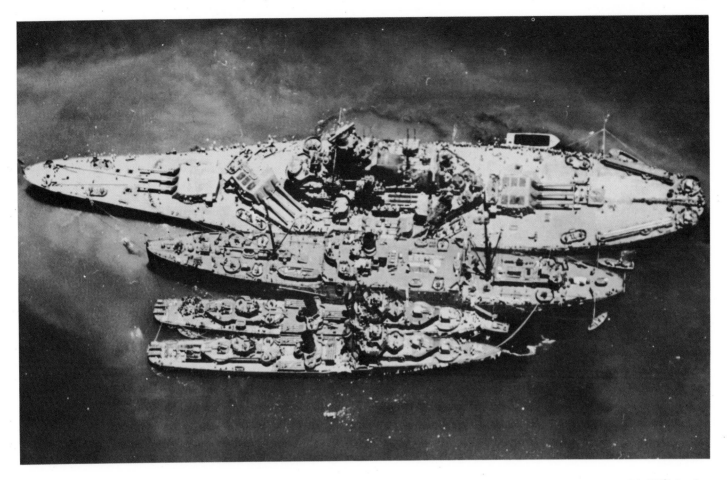

Above: The repair ship *Prometheus* services the battleship USS *South Dakota* and two destroyers damaged in a collision.

much further and hit the destroyer *O'Brien*. She had one of the most remarkable escapes of any destroyer in history for the 21-inch torpedo hit her right on the bow and blew it off in a tremendous explosion, but without sinking her or causing any casualties. The *I.15* nearly got the carrier *Hornet* as well, and the lookouts on the bridge of the escorting destroyer *Mustin* were horrified to see a torpedo track passing under their own keel. Fortunately it was this torpedo which hit the *North Carolina*, as a hit on the carrier could have been the knockout blow for the Solomons campaign.

By mid-afternoon the *Wasp* was beyond hope and the firefighting parties were forced to abandon ship; when a violent explosion blew out the midships elevator 20 minutes later Rear-Admiral Scott ordered everybody off. The carrier lay burning for another two hours, with continuing explosions tearing her hull apart. Admiral Scott hoped to get firefighting parties aboard later, but at 1745 Rear-Admiral Noyes ordered the scuttling of his former flagship. The destroyer *Lansdowne* had the melancholy job of sinking the *Wasp* with four torpedoes. The *O'Brien* managed to limp to Noumea for emergency repairs, but an estimate of her seaworthiness by repair staff of the destroyer tender based there proved to be over-optimistic, and on 19 October her badly strained hull broke up off Samoa, one of the rare examples of structural failure in destroyers.

The 'Tokyo Express' was still running and it became one of the outstanding achievements of the Imperial Japanese Navy. Without the benefit of radar, the Japanese had still achieved a proficiency in night-fighting shown to overwhelming advantage off Savo Island. After the first battle Admiral Mikawa sent Rear-Admiral Raizo Tanaka and his 2nd Destroyer Flotilla to run 900 troops to Guadalcanal, and the success of this operation led to further attempts. On most evenings, just before nightfall, a force of destroyers or other small warships would leave Rabaul and dash down the 'Slot' between New Georgia and Santa Isabel, arriving off Guadalcanal about midnight. The troops and supplies were landed at Cape Esperance or Tassafaronga, and then

the 'Tokyo Express' headed southeast to bombard Henderson Field, and then about one and one-half hours after arrival, they were homeward bound. At daybreak the sweating and cursing Marine Corps would fill in the holes in the airstrip to allow the defending fighters to take off, but once night fell the Japanese Navy was once again in command.

It was 'Tenacious Tanaka' (his nickname was bestowed by his reluctant Marine Corps admirers) who was leading the transports in the light cruiser *Jintsu* in the Battle of the Eastern Solomons on 24 August. When his flagship was damaged by a bomb he transferred to the destroyer *Kagero*. On the night of 4–5 September Tanaka's destroyers sank the flush-deckers *Gregory* and *Little* off Lunga Point with gunfire before escaping. The Japanese did not have it all their own way, and on the night of 11–12 October an attempt to repeat the success of Savo Island by bringing heavier forces down the 'Slot' brought on the disastrous Battle of Cape Esperance. This time the Americans were waiting; Admiral Scott's Task Force 64 was plotting Admiral Aritomo Goto's path on radar.

The Americans had learned by their mistakes, and although their estimate of Goto's force underestimated its strength the sighting reports were passed rapidly to Admiral Scott's Task Force 'Sugar' guarding the approach to Ironbottom Sound.

The battle which followed was confused to say the least. Admiral Scott had the tactical advantage over Goto's cruisers, and managed to cross his T. The four cruisers went into action as planned but three of their four destroyers got out of station and found themselves between the two opposing battle-lines. As a result Admiral Scott ordered a ceasefire to avoid what he thought was an attack on his own forces, but Admiral Goto was equally confused, and thought that he too was being fired on by his own side. But it was American gunfire which hit the flagship

Aoba and mortally wounded it and Admiral Goto. The destroyer *Duncan* had been hit, possibly by an American shell but Lieutenant-Commander Taylor continued an attack which he was making on the heavy cruiser *Furutaka*. Just as she fired two torpedoes she was hit by another American salvo which crippled her, and she sheered off in flames, nearly out of control. The USS *Farenholt* was also hit by her own side, but she survived a shell in the forward fire-room and crawled out of range.

The Japanese destroyer *Fubuki* came within a mile of the heavy cruiser *San Francisco*, a range at which the 8-inch shells sank her in minutes. The cause of her loss was a turn by the heavy cruiser *Furutaka*, and she too ran into the American cruisers' concentration fire. Although soon ablaze from end to end she stayed afloat for about another hour. Next day two more Japanese destroyers, the *Murakumo* and *Natsagumo* were sunk by Henderson Field's dive-bombers, making the Japanese losses for the battle three destroyers and a heavy cruiser sunk, and two more cruisers damaged, at a cost of one US destroyer sunk and one destroyer and two cruisers damaged.

The Japanese were so galled by the air strikes of the Marine Corps pilots from Henderson Field that only a day later they sent the fast battleships *Haruna* and *Kongo* to shell the airstrip. This caused so much disruption that the following night, 14–15 October, Tanaka's destroyers ran a convoy of five transports into Tassafaronga, bringing 4500 fresh troops and large quantities of ammunition and food for the defenders. The previous night nearly a thousand 14-inch shells had landed on Henderson Field; this time the airstrip was pitted with hits from nearly as many 8-inch shells. However, the invaders were holding their own against furious attacks, and the vital airfield remained in the Marines' tenacious grip. The strain was almost intolerable, with air attacks by day and bombardments by night. Another attempt to loosen the US Navy's grip resulted in the Battle of the Santa Cruz Islands on 26 October in which the opposing carrier air groups did most of the fighting, and the destroyers could do little but watch. The major casualty was the USS *Hornet* which was set on fire by four bombers early in the battle.

During the first two weeks of November Tanaka's destroyers continued to run the 'Tokyo Express,' with over 60 missions. The Americans were also exerting every effort to bring in convoys, and the respective covering forces clashed in the action known as the Battle of Guadalcanal. For the superstitious the date, Friday 13 November, was a bad omen, and so it turned out. It was the Japanese who arrived first, Vice-Admiral Hiroaki Abe's Striking Force of two battleships, a cruiser and 16 destroyers were sent, all to get Tanaka's 12 destroyers and 11,000 men through.

Against this the Americans could only put Rear-Admiral Daniel J Callaghan's Task Group 67.4, five cruisers and eight

destroyers, although the battleships *South Dakota* and *Washington* and the carrier *Enterprise* were a day's steaming away. It was a savage mêlée, and lack of radio-discipline completely cancelled out the American Squadron's advantage of radar. The TBS net was jammed with calls for ranges, bearings, tactical orders, anything which would avert the catastrophe which was fast approaching.

The cruiser *Atlanta* opened fire with her 5-inch guns at 1600 yards, but in return a hurricane of fire swept her as the disciplined Japanese gun-crews swung into their night-fighting drill. A shell on the bridge killed Admiral Norman Scott and all but one of his staff, and soon after she was stopped by torpedo-hits. The destroyers were equally bewildered by the sudden loss of cohesion, and found themselves in a welter of ships charging about firing at one another. The *Barton* had to go hard astern to avoid colliding with her target, but as she did so a brace of torpedoes hit her and broke her in half. The *Cushing*, *Laffey*, *O'Bannon* and *Sterrett* found themselves taking on the battleship *Hiei*, and even fired their 5-inch guns at her. The *Cushing* was slowed down by hits from the *Hiei*'s secondary armament and when the battleship sheered off into the smoke-haze, Japanese destroyers came up to finish her with gunfire. The *Laffey* fired two torpedoes at the *Hiei* so close that the watchers on the bridge saw the two 'fish' bounce out of the water after hitting the battleship's 'bulge' without exploding. Retribution was swift, and within seconds the *Laffey* was hit by 1400-pound shells and a torpedo, which left her shattered and killed nearly her entire crew. For his determined bravery Lieutenant-Commander W E Hank was awarded the Navy Cross posthumously.

The *Sterrett* and *O'Bannon* found themselves on the opposite side of the *Hiei* and probably benefited from the distraction offered by the *Cushing* and *Laffey*'s destruction. At one moment the *O'Bannon* found herself so close to the *Hiei* that, just like the *Spitfire* and the *Nassau* at Jutland, the 14-inch guns could not depress low enough to hit the destroyer. The *Sterrett* was roughly handled by two of the *Hiei*'s escorting destroyers, but she also lived to tell the tale. The *Monssen* also ran into a group of destroyers with the *Hiei*, but she did not escape. She was overwhelmed by gunfire and set ablaze from end to end; some 130 men died in the inferno, although three heroic crewmen reboarded her and rescued some of the wounded. Other destroyers were damaged in the witches' sabbath that night, but the worst was over for them. Admiral Callaghan, whose confusing and contradictory orders had been a prime cause of the carnage, was killed on the bridge of his flagship, the heavy cruiser *San Francisco*, by gunfire from the *Kirishima*. The *Hiei* was hit by 8-inch shells from the American cruisers, and was seen to make a half-circle turn and stagger north along the east side of Savo

Below: USS *O'Bannon* in 1942. She distinguished herself in the Battle of Guadalcanal in November 1942 when she took part in a destroyer attack on the battleship *Hiei*.

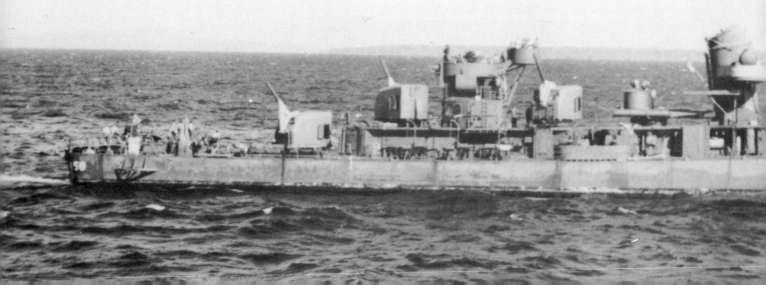

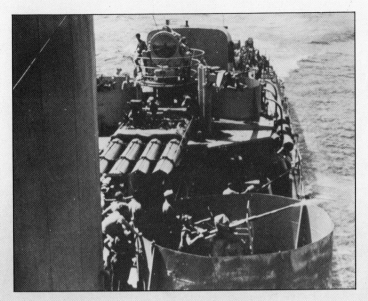

Above: The forward torpedo tubes and a 20-mm antiaircraft gun of USS *Jouett* (DD.396).

Island. At about 1100 next morning the battered cruiser squadron ran into the Japanese submarine *I.26*'s patrol area, and in spite of a depth-charge attack by the *Sterrett* her torpedoes hit the antiaircraft cruiser *Juneau*. The magazines must have been detonated and the ship blew up with the loss of all but 10 of her 700-strong crew.

The second act of the drama unfolded the following night when the American reinforcements had arrived. Four destroyers, the *Benham*, *Gwin*, *Preston* and *Walke* were escorting the battleships *South Dakota* and *Washington* which were positioned off Savo Island to intercept Vice-Admiral Kondo's Bombardment Group, the *Kirishima*, four cruisers and nine destroyers. Other targets were the remnants of the latest 'Tokyo Express,' which had been badly mauled that day by the aircraft of the carrier *Enterprise*, but Kondo's force was the more important.

With the radar coverage provided by his flagship *Washington*, Rear-Admiral Willis A Lee picked up Kondo's ships at a range of 16,000 yards, but once again Japanese eyesight and the superb night-glasses provided to their lookouts gave them the first sighting. The *Preston* was hit just after 2322 and 20 minutes later she was sinking from repeated hits. The *Walke* tried to launch torpedoes but was also hit by shells and then torpedoed. She sank a few minutes after the *Preston* and, almost immediately afterwards, the *Benham* was hit by a torpedo. She was later rescued by the *Gwin*, and the two ships began the long crawl back to Espiritu Santo, but the *Benham*'s bulkheads collapsed under the strain some 12 hours later, and she had to be scuttled.

The two battleships had joined in the firing, but the *South Dakota* was soon in trouble when an electrical failure blacked out the ship, including her radar 'eyes.' She blundered past the burning destroyers and nearly got sunk by approaching too close to the Japanese battle-line. But the *Washington*'s salvoes caused great destruction against the *Kirishima* and probably helped to distract her attention from the lumbering *South Dakota*. The *Kirishima* sank later, and Admiral Kondo withdrew to avoid further losses. This still left Tanaka's transports, but these were caught just at the moment that they arrived at Tassafaronga and the destroyer *Meade* was able to inflict heavy losses on the four helpless targets.

Guadalcanal was the US Navy destroyer's equivalent of Jutland, a muddled series of actions in which they covered themselves with glory. There was the same blend of muddle and heroism, with faulty communication causing heavy losses, but also a devotion to duty which went a long way to snatch victory out of defeat. There was another parallel with Jutland, for although the Japanese could boast that they had sunk a lot of USN ships they had finally lost the initiative and were never to regain it.

Tanaka was to have one more success, in the Battle of Tassafaronga on the night of 30 November–1 December 1942. His eight destroyers and fast transports were jumped by Rear-Admiral Carleton H Wright's Task Force 67, but once again Japanese tactics were superior. The US destroyers' torpedoes all missed, whereas four US cruisers were torpedoed, and one later sank. But the 'Tokyo Express' was running out of steam, and the Japanese High Command had come to realize belatedly that they would never expel the Americans from the Solomons. The last runs of the 'Tokyo Express' were made in reverse, evacuating the garrison that had been kept supplied at such a high cost in lives, ships and aircraft. On the night of 1–2 February 1943 a week-long operation started, the lifting of 12,000 soldiers for the loss of only one destroyer. Although Tanaka was no longer in charge it was a fitting tribute to a remarkable destroyer man and the skill of his crews.

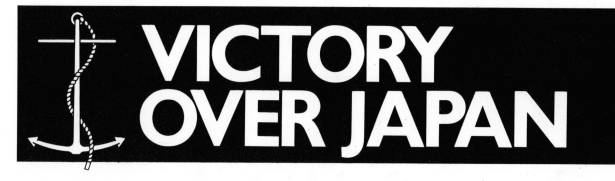

VICTORY OVER JAPAN

The island-by-island campaign to occupy the rest of the Solomons chain after the Marines' hold on Guadalcanal was established was a land, sea and air campaign, but inevitably the destroyers played an essential role, for their speed and torpedo armament made them tough opponents for the Japanese. The battles could be taken as a destroyer's roll of honour, Kula Gulf, Kolombangara, Vella Gulf, Vella Lavella, Empress Augusta Bay and Cape St George, but in addition there were scores of other actions through 1943 in which destroyers fought hard and often.

The first of the new men to rise to prominence was Rear-Admiral W I 'Pug' Ainsworth, who was appointed Commander Destroyers, Pacific (ComDesPac) in June 1942. He had a distinguished career as a destroyer captain, and had been in command of a destroyer squadron in the Atlantic in 1941. Admiral Halsey appointed him to command Task Force 67 after the force had been roughly handled by Tanaka's destroyers in the Battle of Tassafaronga. He showed his mettle by leading a destroyer raid on Munda, at the northwest end of New Georgia, on the night of 4–5 January 1943. For the first time the Americans got the better of the exchange, and it showed that a new spirit of confidence had been generated. In his report Ainsworth said, 'The night bombardment of Munda is . . . the first naval action in which our Navy has coordinated surface, submarine and aircraft units in a night bombardment. As an initial venture in this field of operation, this action may be taken as our first lesson in night amphibious warfare.'

Another exploit of Ainsworth's destroyers was the laying of a minefield right in the path of the 'Tokyo Express' route between Arundel and Kolombangara. The minelayers were three old flush-deckers, the *Breese*, *Gamble* and *Preble*, which had been converted in the 1930s to 'three-stackers' with mine-rails for laying 80 mines. On the night of 6–7 May 1943 the three old destroyers, with the new *Fletcher* Class *Radford* using her radar to act as a guide, laid 250 mines in the middle of Blackett Strait. Admiral Ainsworth covered the operation with three light cruisers and three fleet destroyers. The whole escapade was accomplished without loss, although a Japanese float plane spotted the force as it withdrew. The risks were justified sooner than anticipated, for the next morning four enemy destroyers ran straight into the minefield. In quick succession the *Oyashio*, *Kagero* and *Kurashio* were hit, and only the *Michishio* escaped. Packed with survivors, she was strafed by US aircraft from Guadalcanal which had been called up by one of the Australian coast-watchers. Five days later Admiral Ainsworth's force attempted a similar coup, but a series of mishaps gave away the position of the minefield prematurely, so that the Japanese minesweepers were able to deal with it quickly.

Ainsworth's Task Group 36 met the Japanese headlong in the Battle of Kula Gulf on the night of 5–6 July. Once again it was a confused battle in typical Solomons conditions, a moonless and humid night with visibility up to two miles but liable to be reduced by sudden rain squalls. The Japanese force was a group of 10 destroyers under Rear-Admiral Teruo Akiyama, running supplies to Vila-Stanmore, whereas the Americans had the cruisers *Honolulu*, *Helena* and *St Louis* and DesRon 21, the destroyers *Nicholas*, *Jenkins*, *O'Bannon* and *Radford*. Although the Japanese were outnumbered, four of their destroyers were of a new and powerful type known as the *Akizuki* Class, and one of these, the flagship *Niizuki* had the new Type 22 radar set. As all 10 also had the 24-inch 'Long Lance' torpedoes with reloads the American advantage of fire-power was not as great as it looked on paper.

Although the Japanese lookouts saw the American column at a range of about 7000 yards American gunnery was good, and the first salvo of 6-inch shells from the cruisers crippled Akiyama's flagship *Niizuki*. The *Suzukaze* and *Tanikaze* were hit by apparently 'dud' torpedoes, and when their own torpedoes

Below: The Japanese destroyer *Sagiri* in 1931, shortly after being modernized.

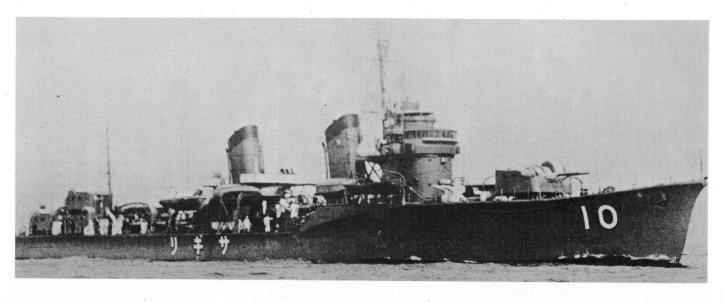

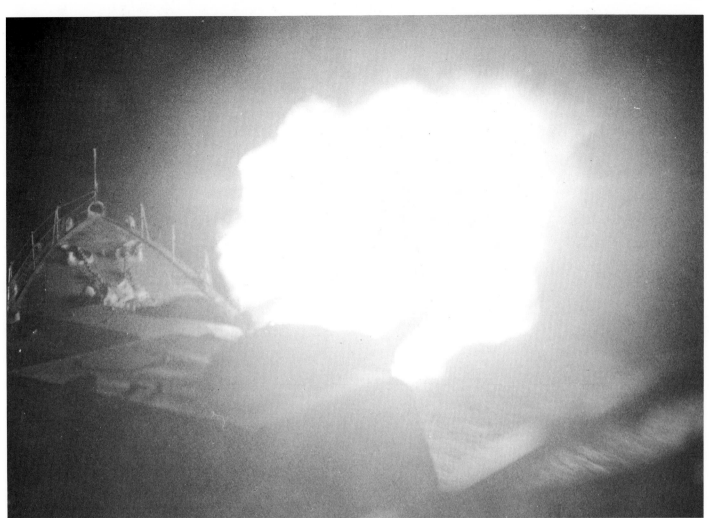

missed they turned away behind their smoke-screen to reload. This time one of the salvoes ran straight, and the three 'Long Lances' which ripped into the cruiser *Helena* broke her back. So furious was the action by this time that the Admiral and his captains failed to notice what had happened, and did not know until the stricken ship failed to answer her call-sign. Ainsworth kept his formation under control and achieved a crossing of the enemy's T, but once again the torpedoes failed dismally and the *Hatsayuki* was hit by three 'duds.' In this first phase the American tactics had been sound but the enormous advantage conferred by the 'Long Lance' got the Japanese out of trouble.

In the second phase the US destroyers made contact once more and inflicted damage on two enemy ships. The *Nagatsuki* was so badly damaged that she later had to be beached near Vila where she was destroyed by bombing. The *Nicholas* and *Radford* were in the middle of rescuing survivors of the *Helena* when they sighted the *Amagiri* which was on a similar errand of mercy for the *Niizuki* survivors. Having chased her off the two destroyers returned to the job of rescue, only to be interrupted again by the *Mochizuki*. Lieutenant Commander Hill took the *Nicholas* off at full speed followed by the *Radford*, leaving their boats to continue picking up survivors. The *Mochizuki* having been chased away, they returned and picked up their boats before rejoining Admiral Ainsworth.

The results of the battle were disappointing, but they showed that the Japanese could no longer count on getting the first blow in. The loss of the *Helena* was hardly offset by the sinking of the *Niizuki*, but the loss of Admiral Akiyama was another blow to Japanese morale. Unfortunately the Battle of Kolombangara a week later showed the dangers of using cruisers against the Japanese destroyers. Once again ships were hit at ranges previously thought impossible for torpedo attack, and

Above: In a night action a destroyer's 5-inch 38 caliber guns give a dramatic flash.

the cruisers *Leander* (New Zealand), *Honolulu* (Ainsworth's flagship) and *St Louis* were hit. The Japanese light cruiser *Jintsu* was destroyed, killing Admiral Izaki and nearly 500 of her crew, and the attempt to get supplies through to the defenders of Vila – Stanmore was frustrated this time. The *Gwin*, the only destroyer which had survived the battleship action at Guadalcanal, was hit by a single torpedo toward the end of the action. With the help of her squadron-mate, *Ralph Talbot*, she was still afloat nearly seven hours later but desperately wounded. US aircraft from airfields in the Russell Islands provided cover against marauding Japanese bombers while the destroyermen labored to save what was now only a smouldering hulk. At about 0900 the commander of DesDiv 23, Commander Higgins, decided that nothing further could be done, and ordered her to be scuttled.

The second name to rise to fame in the Solomons was that of Commander Frederick Moosbrugger, who had been given command of DesDiv 12 at Tulagi. When Munda fell at the beginning of August 1943 he was given the job of intercepting another 'Tokyo Express' run in Gizo Strait supported by fighter cover and PT-Boats. Flying his flag in the *Dunlap*, he had the *Craven* and *Maury* under him as well as DesDiv 15, the destroyers *Lang*, *Stack* and *Sterrett*. On the night of 5–6 August the two divisions steamed north of Vella Gulf, between Vella Lavella and Kolombangara. First contact was obtained by the *Dunlap* on radar at 2333 and only minutes later Moosbrugger gave the order via TBS (the Talk Between Ships short range radio net). 'Stand by to fire torpedoes.' The range came down to 1000 yards and for once the

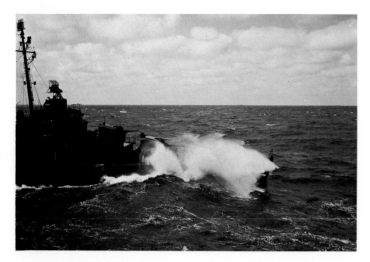

Above: A *Fletcher* Class destroyer heads towards Japan in 1945.

Japanese seem to have been taken completely by surprise. Within minutes the *Kawakaze* sank after four torpedo-hits from the *Stack*. The *Arashi* and *Hagikaze* blew up leaving only the *Shigure* to make her escape at high speed back to Bougainville. This was the Battle of Vella Gulf and it was unusual in that the US Navy suffered no losses at all. But this was not accidental, for Moosbrugger had insisted that his destroyers did not use the unreliable magnetic exploder on their torpedoes' warheads; instead the old and trusted 'contact' setting was used. Another improvement was the fitting of flash-guards to the lips of the torpedo-tubes to reduce the risk of the flash of the cordite impulse-charge being seen by Japanese lookouts as the torpedoes were fired.

The upshot of all these confused and deadly night actions was the cancelling of the 'Tokyo Express' on the orders of the new Japanese Commander in Chief, Admiral Koga. This meant that the outlying garrisons had to be ferried back to Bougainville in landing barges, and so a tempting 'soft-skinned' target was presented to the commander of DesDiv 12 and his fellow destroyer commanders. Between 9 August and 4 October the destroyer squadrons sank some 40 landing barges and escorting gunboats and other light craft. The carnage forced Admiral Koga to reform the 'Tokyo Express,' and this quickly brought on another action, the Battle of Vella Lavella, on the night of 6–7 October. This time honors were more even, for three US destroyers took on six Japanese and each side lost one ship to torpedoes. Unfortunately the *O'Bannon* damaged herself by ramming the sinking *Chevalier* in the confusion, but the *Selfridge* managed to limp home after taking a torpedo-hit.

Captain Arleigh A Burke rose to prominence as a result of his leadership of DesRon 23 in the Battle of Empress Augusta Bay on the night of 2 November 1943. The Japanese had despatched the heavy cruisers *Myoko* and *Haguro*, the light cruisers *Sendai* and *Agano* and six destroyers to cover a force of five fast transports heading for Cape Torokina. The American Admiral Merrill was flying his flag in the light cruiser *Montpelier*, with her sisters *Cleveland*, *Columbia* and *Denver* and eight destroyers of Burke's DesDiv 45 and Commander B L Austin's DesDiv 46. It is interesting to note that Merrill's answer to the menace of the 'Long Lance' was to allow his destroyers to attack with torpedoes first to force the Japanese to keep their distance, and then use radar-assisted long-range gunfire to keep the advantage on his side. Unfortunately a turnaway by the Japanese squadron meant that DesDiv 45's torpedoes all missed. As soon as Admiral Merrill realized that the Japanese had spotted his cruisers he countermanded his original plan and ordered the cruisers to open fire. The cruiser *Sendai* reeled under the impact of a number of 6-inch shell hits and in the confusion the destroyers *Samidare* and *Shiratsuya* collided with one another.

The Americans also had their problems. The destroyer *Foote* lost station, was hit in the stern by a Japanese torpedo, and then narrowly escaped being run down by the cruiser *Cleveland*. The *Spence* and *Thatcher* swung together with a crash and sparks flew as the two steel hulls ground side by side at 30 knots. The mishap caused no serious damage to either destroyer but at that moment the enemy heavy cruisers *Haguro* and *Myoko* appeared only 4000 yards away and in the excitement it was assumed that they were American so no torpedoes were fired. The mistake was understandable and shortly afterwards there was classic exchange between Austin and Burke over the TBS:
Austin: 'We've just had another close miss. Hope you are not shooting at us.'
Burke: 'Sorry but you'll have to excuse the next four salvoes. They're already on their way.'

This misunderstanding had no ill-effects, and when one of Austin's destroyers, the *Spence*, found that she had too little ammunition to finish off the disabled *Hatsukaze*, Burke's division was called up to complete the task. The destroyers were straining on the leash to pursue the Japanese, but Admiral Merrill wisely ordered them to fall back on his cruisers once more, with the result that they escaped damage from a determined air attack next morning.

Arleigh Burke was soon christened '31-knot Burke' and the 'cans' of Destroyer Squadron 23 were known as the 'Little Beavers' from their unofficial insignia. The flagship was the *Fletcher* Class *Charles Ausburne*, which won 11 Battle Stars in three years. Burke's nickname was won in November 1943, when DesRon 23 was refuelling at Hathorn Sound in Kula Gulf. Orders came through to steam at top speed to intercept a Japanese convoy evacuating air force personnel, and the *Charles Ausburne* confirmed that she and her three squadron-mates would make the arranged rendezvous by a specified time. Back at Admiral Halsey's head-quarters the operations officer worked out the average speed needed for the run as 31 knots and remembered that Burke had recently insisted that his squadron could only make a maximum formation speed of 30 knots. Admiral Halsey's next order to Burke read:
'Thirty-one knot Burke get athwart the Buka-Rabaul evacuation line about 35 miles west of Buka X. If no enemy contacts by 0300 . . . 25th . . . come south to refuel same place X. If enemy contacted you know what to do.'

The result was the Battle of Cape St George, fought in the early hours of 25 November 1943 between the *Charles Ausburne*, *Dyson*, *Claxton*, *Converse* and *Spence* and the Japanese *Onami*, *Makinami*, *Amagiri*, *Yugiri* and *Uzuki*. In Burke's own words the moonless night was ideal 'for a nice quiet torpedo attack,' and so it proved. The first attack hit two Japanese destroyers, the *Onami* and *Makinami*, and then the American destroyers settled down to a long stern chase as the remaining three enemy destroyers fled to the north. Such was Burke's instinct for destroyer tactics that after 15 minutes he suddenly ordered his squadron to swing to starboard to avoid a possible torpedo attack. As the five destroyers swung back on to their original course three Long Lances exploded astern, detonated either at the end of their run or by running into the wakes of DesRon 23. Under such circumstances it is hardly surprising that the 'Little Beavers' came to regard themselves as a lucky formation, and they responded by adding the *Yugiri* to their night's score.

The struggle for the Solomons was over and the destroyers had contributed greatly toward that achievement. From the first days of trial and error, when the Japanese destroyers and cruisers held the whip hand, destroyers had done all the hardest fighting. Their losses had been heavy but gradually they had

Top right: Antiaircraft armament became increasingly important as the war drew to a close and the Japanese began to employ kamikaze tactics. Seen here is USS *O'Bannon*'s after 20-mm battery.
Center right: USS *Shannon* (DM.25) seen here off Okinawa in 1945.
Below right: USS *Ellyson* was converted to a fast minesweeper (DMS.19).

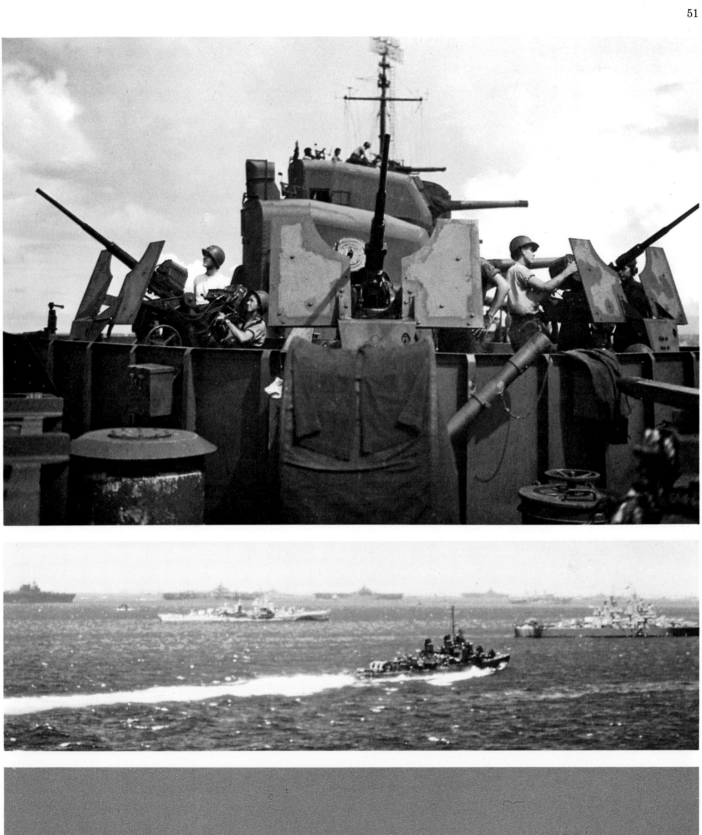

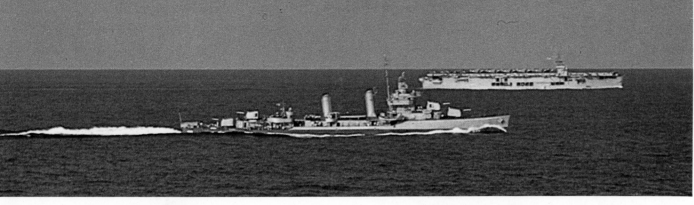

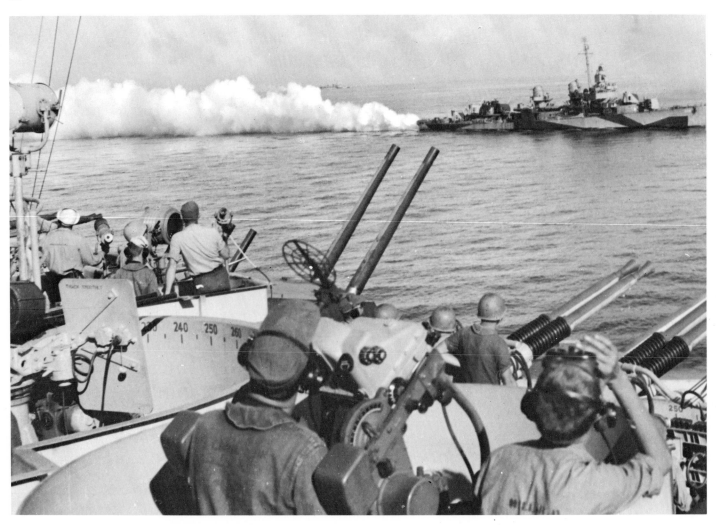

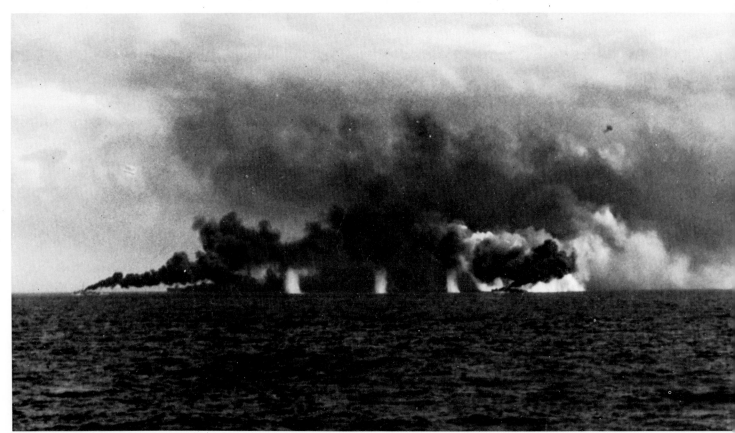

learned to beat the Japanese at their own game, and had become more cunning and resourceful. As one anonymous destroyer-man said, 'in the Solomons everyone felt they were living on borrowed time.'

The American advance across the Central Pacific was comparatively uneventful for the destroyer forces but they came to the fore with the return to the Philippines. The Battle of Leyte Gulf is only a convenient name for a series of four big battles which took place over a period of four days. Together they amount to the greatest sea battle in history and, for the only time in the Pacific, all warship-types played the role for which they had been designed: battleships fought battleships while destroyers attacked with torpedoes and defended their own fleets. It opened with a landing in Leyte Gulf on 20 October 1944, but three days previously the Japanese had initiated their Sho or 'Victory Plan' when they learned that demolition teams and battalions of Rangers had reconnoitered the Leyte beaches. Under the Sho Plan there were four fleets:

1. The Main Body under Vice-Admiral Ozawa, composed of four carriers, two battleship/carrier hybrids, three cruisers and eight destroyers, coming from the Inland Sea.

2. Force A under Vice-Admiral Kurita, composed of five battleships, 12 cruisers and 15 destroyers, coming from Borneo.

3 & 4 Force C, which was in two parts, the Van Squadron under Vice-Admiral Nishimura with two battleships, one cruiser and four destroyers, and the Rear Squadron under Vice-Admiral Shima. This last body included three cruisers and four destroyers, and although both sailed from Borneo they were under separate command.

To the Americans they were known merely by the areas in which they were first spotted, so that the Main Body was labelled the 'Northern Force,' Force A became the 'Center Force' and the two squadrons of Force C became the 'Southern Force.'

Admiral Ozawa and the Northern Force were merely a decoy to lure Halsey's Fast Carrier Task Force away from the invasion area, which in turn would allow Kurita to unite his Center Force with Shima's Southern Force to sweep into Leyte Gulf and destroy the invasion fleet. The Center Force was to reach Leyte Gulf by passing through the San Bernardino Strait between Luzon and Samar and the Southern Force would pass through Surigao Strait between Leyte and Mindanao. Things went wrong on both sides. At first the departure of Ozawa's Northern Force was undetected and so it did not function as a decoy as early as had been hoped. Then Kurita lost three heavy cruisers in an ambush by US submarines off Palawan on 23 October. Next day carrier planes attacked the Center Force and sank the giant battleship *Musashi*, and a temporary turnabout by Kurita was mistaken for a complete withdrawal. As Ozawa's Northern Force had now been located a jubilant Halsey decided that it was the main Japanese striking force and set off in pursuit. At 1512 on 24 October he signalled his intention of forming a new task force of battleships and carriers to guard the exit of the San Bernardino Strait. Although nothing was done about it, the Seventh Fleet, which had the responsibility of guarding the invasion fleet assumed that the task force had been formed and that the exit was guarded. The other exit, Surigao Strait, was guarded by Admiral Jesse Oldendorf's six old battleships and eight cruisers with 20 destroyers in attendance, but the failure to watch the San Bernardino Strait put the entire invasion armada at the mercy of Admiral Kurita's powerful force.

Oldendorf had been warned at midday to expect a night engagement and he had laid a cunning trap. He sent 30 PT Boats forward to give early warning of Nishimura's approach. Further in he put the destroyers of DesRon 54, the *McDermot* and *Monssen* on the right flank and the *Remey*, *Melvin* and *McGowan* on the left flank. Tucked away close to the coastline of Leyte was the third line of defense, the *Hutchins*, *Bache*, *Dale*, *Arunta* (Australian), *Beale* and *Killen* of DesRon 24. The final element of the trap was a double line of five cruisers and six battleships, with the remaining nine destroyers of DesRon 56 in the center. The Strait is 12 miles wide at this point, and so the cruisers were used to extend the patrol line in case the Japanese tried to slip past. Although nothing much was expected of the PT Boats, they were stationed as far down the Strait as possible so that their surface-warning radar sets could give accurate coverage.

The PT Boats made contact at 2230 and although they did

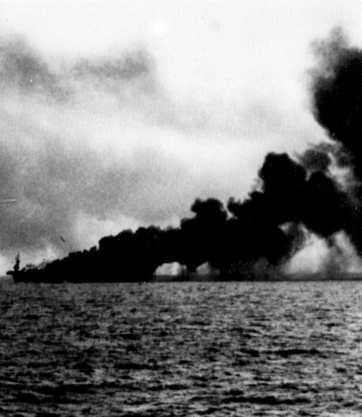

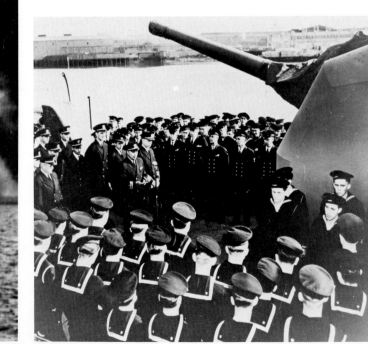

Above left: Smoke laying was an important destroyer task. Here a *Fletcher* Class unit hides a battleship at the Battle of Leyte Gulf, 1944.
Below left: US escort carriers and destroyers under heavy Japanese fire at San Bernadino Strait.
Below: USS *Johnston* (DD.557) being commissioned at Seattle in October 1943.

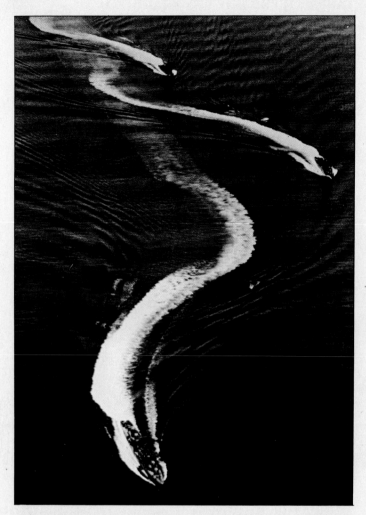

Above: Destroyers of DesRon 23 on maneuvers in the Solomon Islands 1943–44.

their best, the Japanese brushed them aside and steamed on. DesRon 54 did not catch sight of them until 0300 but their first torpedo attacks had no effect either, and they had to retire at high speed, zigzagging and making smoke. But three out of the 47 fired hit, two against the battleship *Fuso*'s side and one against the destroyer *Michishio*. It must have been a majestic sight, four destroyers leading the flagship *Yamashiro*, the *Fuso* and the cruiser *Mogami* at one-kilometer intervals, weaving to dodge the torpedoes and trying to pick off the attacking destroyers in the glare of searchlights.

At 0349 the *Fuso* finally blew up, and the two halves of the battleship drifted crazily down the Strait for some time before sinking. But Nishimura ploughed on doggedly, and his flagship seemed to be impervious to the hail of torpedoes and shells fired at her by DesRon 24. Another destroyer, the *Yamagumo* had been sunk, but still the Japanese advanced. One of DesRon 24's destroyers, the *Killen* is credited with a killing torpedo-hit on *Yamashiro*, for her skipper Commander Corey, decided to order a depth-setting of 22 feet on the torpedoes to inflict maximum damage. The salvo ran straight, but the blazing battleship still careered on towards Oldendorf's waiting battleships. Although the plan was to finish off the Japanese by gunfire some of the destroyers of DesRon 56, held in reserve between the battleships and the cruisers, took a hand in the action. One of their torpedoes hit the destroyer *Asagumo* but the *Albert W Grant* was hit by 6-inch shells from her own side before she could get out of range. In all she was hit by seven Japanese 4.7-inch shells and 11 US 6-inch, and suffered heavy casualties.

It was left to the battleships to administer the *coup de grâce* to the *Yamashiro*, and the tortured battleship finally capsized at 0419. The cruiser *Mogami* and the destroyer *Shigure* fled at high speed, and when Admiral Shima learned of the disaster he withdrew. Air attacks and PT Boats accounted for the cruisers *Abukuma*, *Nachi* and *Mogami* and two of his destroyers, with the result that only three destroyers out of the whole Southern Force survived the Battle of Surigao Strait. The victors emerged almost without a scratch, apart from the sorely tried *Grant*, and even she lived to fight another day.

As Admiral Oldendorf's ships finished their work the news came through of desperate fighting off Samar. Not until 0645 had anyone been able to ascertain the unwelcome news that no

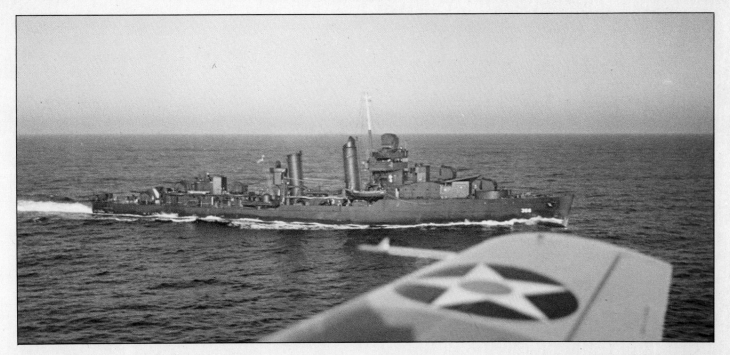

Above: USS *Drayton* (DD.366) sported an unusual camouflage which led to her nickname of 'The Blue Beetle.'
Below: USS *Heerman* (DD.532) laying smoke off Samar, October 1944.

ships were guarding the San Bernardino Strait. In another ten minutes Rear-Admiral Sprague's escort carriers learned the awful truth, as 18-inch shells from the giant battleship *Yamato* began to fall around them, Kurita's Center Force had got within 17 miles of the escort carriers which were providing air cover for the massive fleet of transports and landing craft in Leyte Gulf. The six 'jeep carriers' were escorted by only three destroyers and four DEs, the *Hoel*, *Heermann*, *Johnston*, *Dennis*, *John C Butler*, *Raymond* and *Samuel B Roberts*, and they were all that stood between Kurita and a slaughter of the defenseless transports. The alarm had been sounded and reinforcements were on the way, but they were too far away to be of any immediate help. The DEs were not designed to fight anything but submarines, but fortunately most of the earlier vessels of this type had been completed with a set of triple torpedo-tubes, which gave them some limited offensive capability. In speed and maneuverability, however, they were not in the same class as destroyers, and would not be able to look after themselves so well. As for the escort carriers, their small hulls were built to

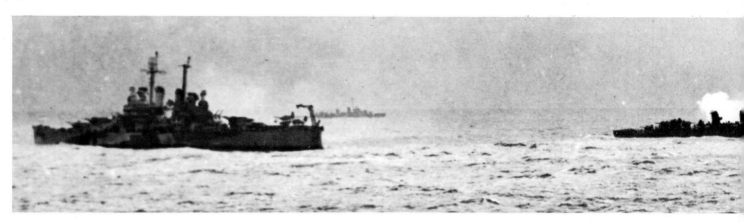

mercantile standards and they were even slower than the DEs, to say nothing of their stores of highly inflammable aviation gasoline.

The *Johnston* under Commander Ernest E Evans found the heavy cruiser *Kumano* within range and rushed to the attack. She launched a salvo of torpedoes but staggered in the water as a salvo hit her. With her speed severely reduced she continued to fire at her opponents, which included the battleship *Kongo*.

She gamely followed the *Hoel* and *Heermann* as they obeyed Admiral Sprague's call for a torpedo attack, but by 0830 her speed was down to 15 knots and only two 5-inch guns were

Below: USS *Hazelwood* (DD.531) attends an *Essex* Class carrier.

firing. The *Johnston* clung to life grimly but the Japanese shells were reducing her to a shambles. Only one shaft was turning, the gyro-compass had been knocked out, and the ship was so helpless that she could not take avoiding action when the *Heermann* collided with her. The *Hoel* (Commander Leon Kintberger) suffered a similar fate, being hit by two of the *Kongo*'s 14-inch shells while racing in to fire her torpedoes. She tried to get clear but found enemy battleships to port and cruisers to starboard. An hour later the destroyer was still afloat after being battered by 40 hits, but when she sank shortly afterward 253 officers and men died. The attack was not in vain as one torpedo hit the 8-inch gunned cruiser *Kumano* and ultimately influenced the outcome of the battle.

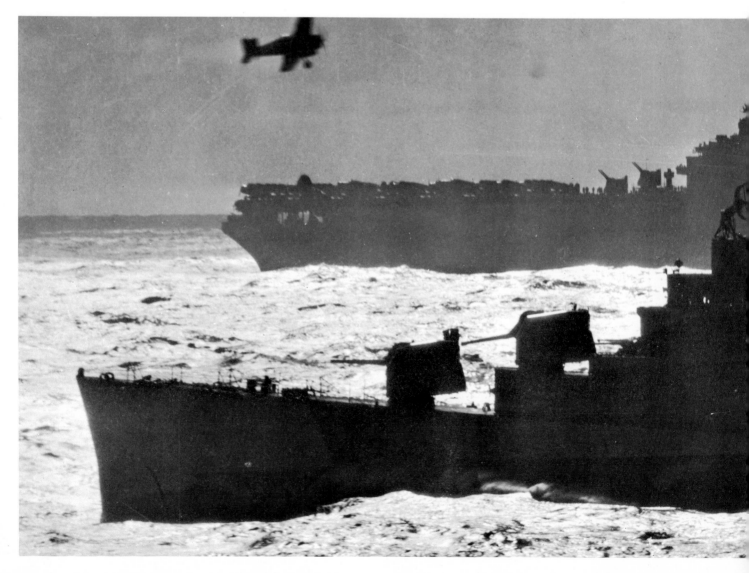

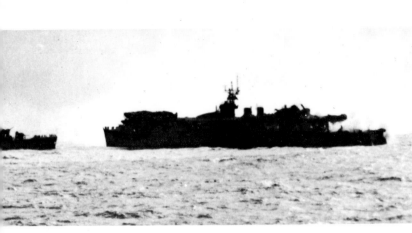

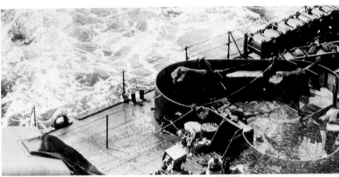

Above: The light cruiser USS *Birmingham* and a *Fletcher* Class
destroyer near the crippled carrier USS *Princeton*.
Right: A Gunners Mate cleans the after 5-inch gun of USS *Brown*
(DD.546) following a night air action off Formosa, October 1944.

Sprague used the code 'men' to signify escort carriers and
'small boys' for his destroyers and destroyer escorts, which
accounts for his next signal:
'Small boys on my starboard quarter interpose with smoke
between men and enemy cruisers.'
The DEs began to lay a smoke-screen but three of them were
ordered to make a torpedo attack as soon as the three destroyers
had finished theirs. The *Samuel B Roberts* was soon hit, but not

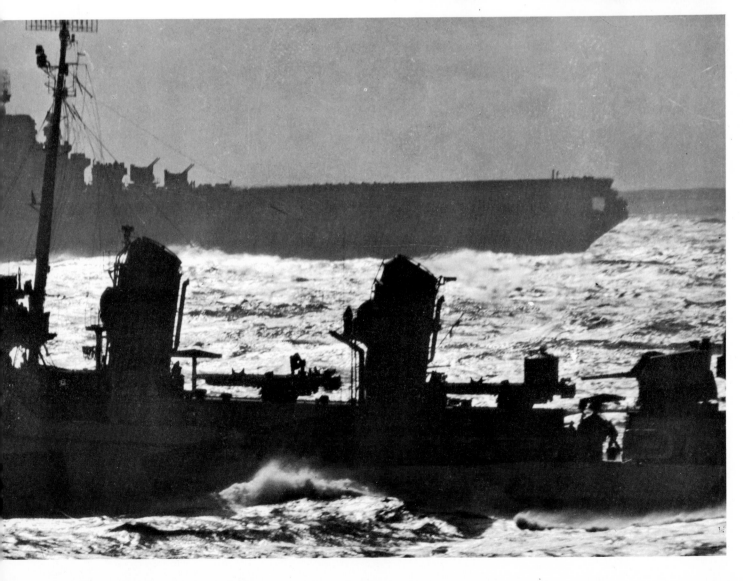

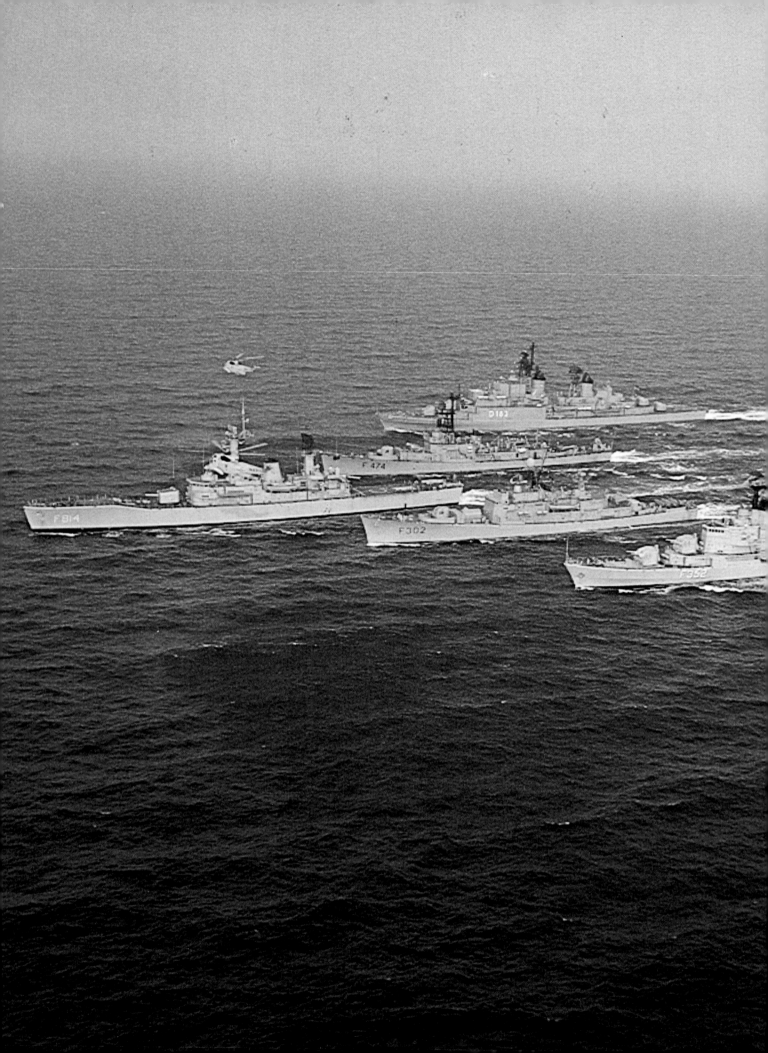

Main picture: Modern destroyers and frigates on NATO maneuvers. Foreground to back: The Danish frigate *Peder Skram* (F.352); the US guided missile destroyer *Coontz* (DDG.40); the Norwegian frigate *Trondheim* (F.302); the Dutch frigate *Isaac Sweers* (F.814); the Canadian helicopter destroyer *Huron* (DDH.281); the Portuguese destroyer *Almirante Megalhaes Correa* (F.474); HMS *Norfolk* (D.21) and the German destroyer *Bayern* (D.138).

Inset left: The USS *Roper* (DD.147) seen here on convoy in 1942 was one of five *Wickes* Class ships converted to fast transports.

Inset right: Checking the 21-inch quintuple torpedo tubes aboard the USS *O'Bannon* in the Pacific in 1943.

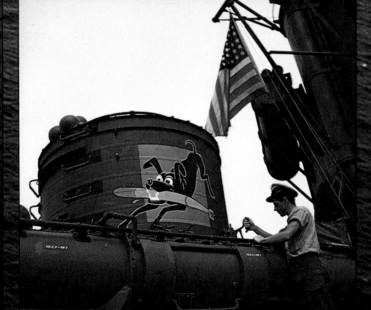

before her salvo of three 'fish' had been fired. Soon her forward 5-inch guns were knocked out, half her armament, but the after gun continued to fire for an hour. Over 300 rounds were fired and even the starshell and practice rounds were fired when nothing else was left. Even though the air-blast had failed, making the gun dangerous to load, the gun-crew continued to load by hand until the heat of the breech 'cooked off' a cordite-charge and wrecked the gun-house.

The *Dennis* was damaged during her torpedo attack, but the *Raymond* escaped, like the *Heermann* before her, with only slight damage. The *John C Butler* was ordered to continue laying the smoke-screen, and the *Dennis* thankfully took cover behind it with the carriers. The carrier *Fanshaw Bay* was hit by four 8-inch shells but they did not stop her. The *Gambier Bay*, however, was hit and set on fire, and had to be abandoned. But the carriers were to undergo a further ordeal, for what Kurita's guns could not achieve, land-based aircraft from Luzon could. At about 2300 the *Saint Lô* and the *Kitkun Bay* were hit by aircraft diving onto their flight decks, a foretaste of the kamikaze attacks to come. The *Kitkun Bay* survived the initial blast

of two Zeroes but later her avgas exploded and tore her flimsy hull apart.

Sprague's small force had been nearly annihilated, but the Japanese never got through to the invasion fleet off Leyte. If there is a chapter in destroyer-operations to match the heroism of Guadalcanal it must surely be the Battle of Samar. With the fate of the entire Philippines campaign depending on them, the seven small ships never flinched.

On the first day of April 1945 a huge invasion force prepared to capture the island of Okinawa in the East China Sea. It was the last step before the invasion of the Japanese Home Islands; possession of the precipitous volcanic island and the rest of the Ryukyu group was vital. Yet, as the bombarding ships 'softened up' the defenders there was an ominous silence.

For Operation Iceberg the US Navy had mustered over 1500 ships, including 40 aircraft carriers and 18 battleships. Most of these were allocated to Admiral Turner's Task Force 51, the Okinawa Expeditionary Force: 10 battleships, 18 escort carriers, eight heavy cruisers, 82 destroyers and 54 destroyer escorts.

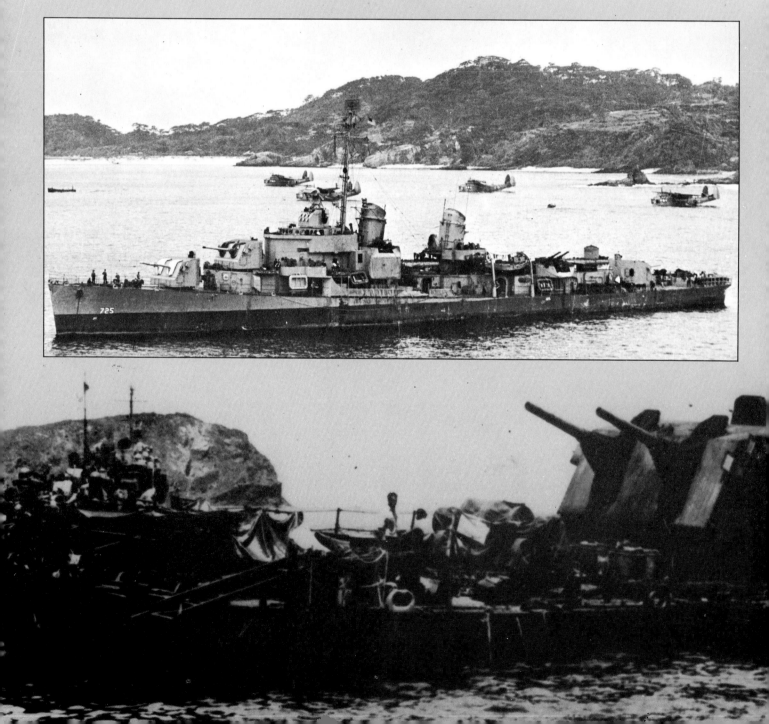

The majority of destroyers and DEs were to screen the invasion area, either by patrolling or maintaining a 'picket line' to give early radar warning of the approach of Japanese aircraft. The threat from kamikazes was known, and it was expected that the Japanese would spare no effort to destroy ships.

The 'radar picket' was an innovation suggested by previous experience, and its purpose was to give early warning of raids by aircraft or surface warships, and in addition to provide fighter-direction. Distant radar pickets were stationed 40–70 miles away from the transport area but there was also a close picket line only 20–25 miles out. There were also destroyers and DEs assigned to radar picket stations in the outer and inner anti-submarine screens. The distant picket line was composed of groups each of which had one Fighter-Director (FD) destroyer and two Landing Craft, Support (LCS) equipped with radar to extend the radar range. The FD destroyers could control any aircraft of the Combat Air Patrol (CAP) assigned to them by the central fighter-direction unit to deal with hostile aircraft in their areas. The force was known as Task Flotilla 5, and it was commanded by Commodore Moosbrugger.

Although the defenders of Okinawa fought tenaciously from the warren of caves and pillboxes on the island, the land fighting was matched by the ferocity of the sea battle. It was soon realized that the main weight of Japanese air attack was falling on the picket line, and that one destroyer to each picket station was not enough. Yet the DEs did not carry enough antiaircraft guns to stand up to continuous air attack. The picket groups were strengthened and eventually comprised three or more destroyers and four LCSs and strenuous efforts were made to keep a CAP over as many stations as possible. As radar stations were established ashore the 16 floating stations were reduced, and after six weeks only five were in use. Another problem was the small number of FD destroyers available and, as ships were damaged or sunk, it became necessary to equip fresh ships as rapidly as possible.

The onslaught on the destroyers began on 6 April, when the *Bush* and *Colhoun* were sunk by kamikaze aircraft. Seven more destroyers and a DE were badly damaged in attacks of an intensity never seen before. The *Colhoun* was hit by no fewer than four kamikazes, but stayed afloat for more than seven hours. The problem of dealing with kamikazes was the human guidance system, which made them in effect operational air-to-surface

Left: Launched in December 1943, USS *O'Brien* (DD.725) had twin five-inch gun mountings and heavy antiaircraft defenses.
Below: The destroyer-minelayer USS *Aaron Ward* (DM.34) still floats after being hit by no less than five kamikazes off Kerama Retto in May 1945.

guided missiles. Once the aircraft had been steered into its final dive the target ship had to destroy it by literally shooting it apart. This the 40mm Bofors antiaircraft gun could not do as it did not fire proximity-fused (VT) ammunition; nor did the five-inch dual-purpose gun fire fast enough to do the job. It was found that the best tactic for destroyers was not to weave and zigzag, as they normally did under air attack, but to remain steady to maintain a good gun-platform as long as possible to give the AA guns the best chance. Destroyers are such lively craft that the motion and vibration of being thrown about at high speed was too much for their fire-control, whereas larger warships could cope with evasive maneuvers with no loss of accuracy.

But all this was academic, for the immediate problem of the destroyers was to survive the 'divine wind' which was striking them down in ever-increasing numbers. Added to the obsolescent aircraft was the Ohka or 'Baka' bomb, a small piloted rocket

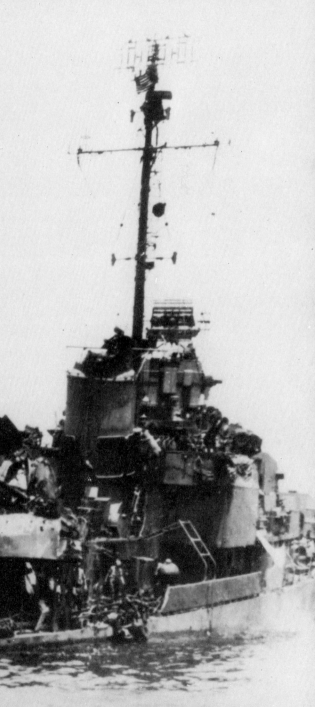

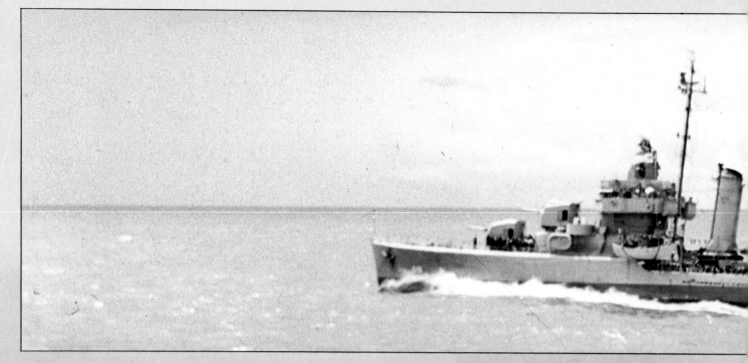

bomb which achieved a diving speed of 535mph. The attacks continued right through to the end of July and, in all, 13 destroyers and DEs were sunk off Okinawa and another 88 damaged. In many instances the casualties were on a terrible scale – as many as a third of the entire complement; in others the loss of life was miraculously light. One of the worst cases was, ironically, not a kamikaze attack. On 18 May the *Longshaw* was on the fifth day of a gruelling routine of fire-support off the beaches when she ran aground on a reef. Japanese shore-batteries ranged on her and began to demolish her methodically until her superstructure was a mass of tangled steel. The captain gave the order to abandon ship, but the casualties continued to mount up. The wrecked destroyer resembled a slaughterhouse, with dead and wounded trapped in every corner. Thirteen officers and 73 enlisted men were killed and 90 wounded.

After the battle was over Moosbrugger paid tribute to his destroyers:

'The performance of the personnel of the screening and radar picket ships, both individually and collectively, was superb through the Okinawa campaign. Acts of heroism and unselfishness, fighting spirit, coolness under fire, unswerving determination, endurance and qualities of leadership and loyalty exceeded all previous conceptions set for the US Navy. The radar picket station groups took every blow that the Japs could inflict and absorbed terrific punishment in personnel casualties and material damage, . . .'

While the American destroyers were locked in their terrible struggle with the kamikazes four British destroyers of the East Indies Fleet fought what turned out to be the last classic destroyer action in history. On 9 May two submarines in the Malacca Strait sighted the heavy cruiser *Haguro*, a destroyer and two patrol craft heading northwest. The small Japanese force was carrying supplies to the Andaman Islands and Vice-Admiral H T C Walker detached escort carriers and the 26th Destroyer Flotilla under Captain Manly Power to search north of Sumatra for it. On the morning of 15 May an aircraft from HMS *Shah* signalled that she had sighted the *Haguro*, and at 2300 that night the flotilla leader HMS *Saumarez* picked up a radar contact at a distance of 34 miles. Captain Power planned his attack with care, ensuring that whichever way the *Haguro* turned she could be caught.

Even at this late stage the Japanese had not lost their boldness, and while the four destroyers were moving into position the cruiser suddenly reversed course. There was a brisk flurry of gunfire during which the *Saumarez* was hit several times. She and HMS *Verulam* fired their torpedoes, and when the *Haguro* turned away to avoid these she ran into the torpedoes from the *Venus* and *Virago*. The cruiser sank just before 0200 on 16 May, about 45 miles southwest of Penang, but her escorting destroyer the *Hamakaze*, escaped and was able to pick up survivors when the 26th Flotilla had left the scene. Although only a minor action it was appropriate that British destroyers should finish

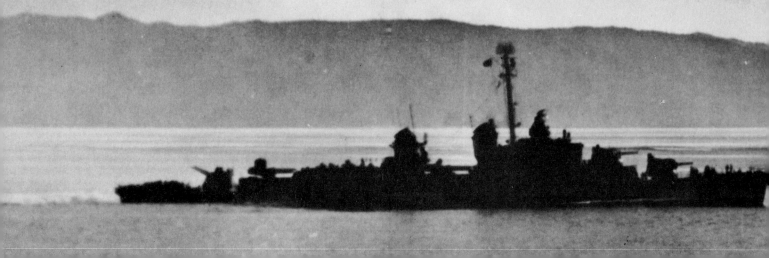

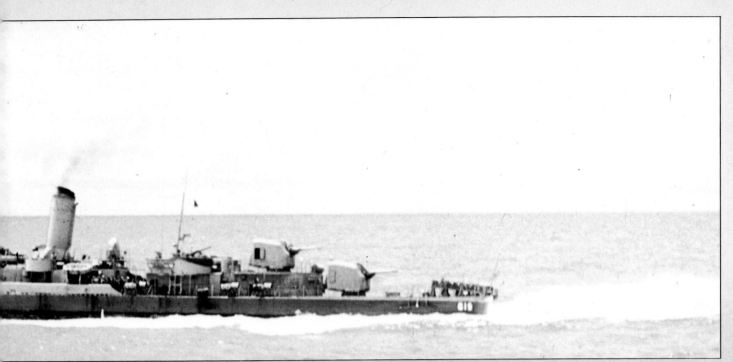

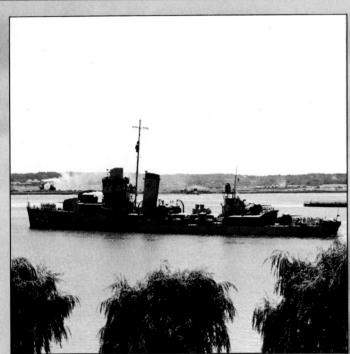

Above: USS *Edwards* (DD.619) of the *Bristol* Class on a shakedown cruise in the Caribbean in 1942.
Left: USS *Trippe* (DD.403) survived World War II only to be used as a target during the atom bomb tests at Bikini Atoll in 1946.
Below: Two *Allen M Sumner* Class destroyers in the Mindanao Sea off the Philippines in January 1945.

their long and distinguished war career with a text-book operation.

It is difficult to establish the last action fought by destroyers but in the European Theater it was probably between German destroyers or torpedo boats and Soviet aircraft as the *Kriegsmarine* struggled to evacuate Eastern Prussia in the face of the Russian advance. On 5 May 1945 the *Hans Lody, Friedrich Ihn, Thoedor Riedel, Z.25, T.17, T.19, T.28* and *T.35* fought off attacks by Soviet motor torpedo boats to escort a convoy with 45,000 refugees to Copenhagen. It was the *Kriegsmarine*'s swansong, and as at Dunkirk and Guadalcanal, destroyers bore the brunt. In the Pacific, the situation was similar but on a much larger scale as US carrier aircraft wiped out the remnants of the Imperial Japanese Navy in each and every anchorage. The last amphibious landing was in Borneo, and on 30 June, just six weeks before the surrender, US destroyers fired 18,820 rounds of 5-inch ammunition at Balikpapan. It was appropriate that they should be at the scene of DesDiv 59's heroic action in January 1942.

INDEX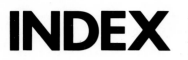

Page numbers in italics
refer to illustrations

Acknowledgments

The author would like to thank
David Eldred, the designer,
R. Watson who compiled the
index and Richard Natkiel who
prepared the maps. The
following agencies supplied the
illustrations:

Bison: p 19 (top)
Collezione Aldo Fraccarole:
pp 28 (top), 31
Conway Picture Library:
pp 21 (center), 25 (below)
Foto Drüppel: p 34 (top)
S Fukui: p 36 (above)
Robert Hunt Library: pp 7
(top), 8–9 (all three), 10 (all
three), 12, 14–15 (below),
16–17 (below), 17 (top), 18–19
(below), 20 (top), 22–23 (below),
26–27 (below), 28–29 (below),
30, 32 (all three), 38, 39 (both),
45
Imperial War Museum:
pp 6–7 (bottom), 23 (top)
Mainichi: p 48
Ministry of Defence: p 20–21
(below), 58–59 (main pic),
59 (left)
Musée de la Marine: p 26 (top)
National Archives: pp 40 (top),
49, 53 (top), 54–55 (bottom),
56–57 (bottom), 60–61 (below)
National Maritime Museum:
pp 13 (bottom right), 14 (top),
21 (top)
Maps © Richard Natkiel:
pp 25, 41
US Navy: pp 13 (bottom left),
15 (top), 16 (above), 24, 26
(center), 33 (above), 34–35
(below), 35 (center and right),
36–37 (below), 40–41, 42 (all
three), 44, 46–47 (below), 47
(top), 50, 51 (all three), 52–53,
54 (top), 55 (top), 56–57 (top),
59 (bottom right), 60 (above),
62–63 (all three)